D

Conservatism

Daniel Woodley

**Advanced
Topic*Master***

Series editor
Eric Magee

Philip Allan Updates
Market Place
Deddington
Oxfordshire
OX15 0SE
Tel: 01869 338652
www.philipallan.co.uk

ISBN-10 1-84489-602-1
ISBN-13 978-1-84489-602-8

Printed by Raithby, Lawrence & Co Ltd, Leicester

Environmental information
The paper on which this title is printed is sourced from mills using wood from managed, sustainable forests.

P00688

Contents

Introduction

This book deals in detail with one of the core topics in Unit 4 and Unit 6 of the Edexcel Political Ideas and Doctrines specification. It is also relevant for students taking the AQA Political Ideologies module, as well as students studying the OCR paper on Political Ideas and Concepts. The text is written in a clear and accessible format and is broken down into thematic sections, designed to give students valuable extra insight into the history and theory of conservative thought. Although the book is aimed at more advanced students, it will be of help to all students seeking to develop their AO1 and AO2 skills.

The text is divided into five chapters, each dealing with an overarching question. The aim is for students to build their specialist knowledge and understanding of the sometimes difficult material by following the argument as it unfolds in each chapter. Specially designed tasks have been added at the end of each chapter to test knowledge and understanding, and these should be attempted once the chapter has been read in full. There are also suggestions for further reading at the end of each chapter, and handy links to relevant websites, which students may wish to consult for further discussion of key issues.

Chapter 1 introduces the origins of conservatism as a school of political thought that has its roots in the reaction to the growth of the liberal-rationalist ideas of the Enlightenment in the nineteenth century. The chapter deals with one of the key problems in the conservative tradition, namely whether conservatism should be viewed — like socialism or anarchism — as a systematic political doctrine, or whether it really ought to be viewed as a disposition or state of mind.

In chapter 2, two central concepts in conservative thought are examined and their importance evaluated. All conservatives have an attachment to authority and tradition, but this is often expressed in different ways. For example, modern neo-liberal New Right thinkers value the stabilising power of tradition, but are sceptical of those of a more traditionalist cast who reject all forms of rationalism as inconsistent with the historical continuity and social stability of societies. Again, the chapter deals with an overarching question, and students should take special note of the key evaluation points in the text.

Chapter 3 is devoted to the place of the individual in conservative thought, and differentiates between 'organicist' and 'individualist' currents in different forms of conservative ideology. Like chapter 2, this chapter will be particularly useful for those students seeking to advance their knowledge of conservative theory for

Unit 4 of the Edexcel paper, which regularly includes short answer questions and essays on the relationship between conservatism and individualism.

The purpose of chapter 4 is to provide students with a firm understanding of the origins and development of New Right ideology, focusing in detail on the arguments within the libertarian conservative tradition in favour of economic liberalism and free market capitalism. The text also deals with the problem of the state in New Right thinking, and is designed to show students why modern conservative thinkers and politicians promote the market rather than the state as a more efficient means for allocating resources.

Finally, in chapter 5, one of the key questions in modern British politics is addressed — namely, are the UK Conservatives still to all intents and purposes a 'conservative' political party? This chapter will be particularly useful for those students tackling the conservatism topic in Unit 6 of the Edexcel paper, as well as those who want to understand the impact Thatcherism exerted on the development of British politics (including the ideological development of New Labour). The chapter concludes with an assessment of recent developments in the Conservative Party, following the election of David Cameron as leader.

Daniel Woodley

Conservatism: ideology or disposition?

Introduction

Conservatism is based on a desire to defend the existing social order. Conservatives celebrate the 'accumulated wisdom of the past' and claim to be opposed to radical change and social upheaval, believing these to be detrimental to the continuity and stability of state and society. Yet there is some disagreement among philosophers and social scientists about whether to describe conservatism as a political *doctrine* or simply as a general *disposition*. What does this mean?

We tend to depict someone as conservative if they hold 'traditional' views, if they prefer 'conventional' ways of doing things, and if they dislike 'new' or 'modern' ideas. This is generally what we mean when we use the term 'conservative' with a small 'c'. For example, we might say that older people tend to be more conservative than teenagers because they feel threatened by the rapid pace of change. Similarly, we might say that individuals brought up in more traditional or religious societies are likely to be more conservative and reactive as a result of exposure to specific moral teachings.

On the other hand, political conservatism represents a distinctive set of beliefs and ideas that draw on, but are by no means restricted to, conventional or traditional ways of thinking and being. Political conservatives may defend conventional or traditional ways of thinking and being, but conservative political ideologies are based on more explicit criteria, such as defence of private property, support for organised authority, faith in the institutions of the free market and opposition to permissive social values.

It might be argued that we can draw the same distinction between 'liberalism' in general and 'political liberalism' in particular. Liberals in general believe in individualism, personal freedom, pluralism and toleration, while liberal politicians (such as the Liberal Democrats in the UK) focus on specific issues such as human rights, the environment, education and social reform. In this sense, political liberalism is an organised and explicit expression of a more general liberal outlook, which may vary from one society to another, or between different epochs.

Some conservatives maintain that conservatism is defined by its opposition to the concept of **ideology**, which they see as sets of fashionable political ideas articulated by liberal and socialist intellectuals to mobilise their support base behind reformist or radical agendas. Conservative thinkers such as Michael Oakeshott (1901–90) and Roger Scruton (1944–) stress that conservatism is really a question of temperament not doctrine, but this view can be challenged if we examine the origins of modern conservatism as a political response to liberal rationalism.

In order to determine whether conservatism is an ideology or a disposition we need to examine:

- the origin of conservative ideas in nineteenth-century Europe in opposition to the social and political ideals of the Enlightenment
- the ways in which conservatism (in its many forms) fulfils some or all of the main functions of ideology

Where do conservative ideas originate?

Modern conservatism emerged in the nineteenth century in reaction to the political and social changes associated with the French Revolution and the Industrial Revolution. These epochal events radically altered the social and political landscape of Europe, placing economic power in the hands of a new social class, the bourgeoisie. Although the development of conservatism in different countries testifies to the importance of cultural differences, there are sufficient similarities between different conservative political traditions to allow some degree of generalisation.

The central feature of all conservative ideologies is a reaction against modernity, based on an unwillingness to accept the secular principles of Enlightenment reason. In political terms, the key targets of conservative political ideology are liberal rationalism and statist socialism, which are blamed for promoting radical ideas such as individualism and egalitarianism. For conservatives, such radical ideas are not only inconsistent with human nature, but also undermine the evolutionary structure of established human communities. Defenders of the idea that conservatism is really just a disposition stress the point that it is an anti-ideological way of thinking. Unlike liberalism and socialism, conservatism seeks only to preserve existing or established ways of thinking and being, rather than to theorise or invent new ones.

Students need to understand clearly the intellectual origins of conservatism: in particular, why early conservative thinkers oppose so vehemently the abstract rationalism of the Enlightenment and the ideology of political revolution and transformation bequeathed by the French Revolution.

Opposition to Enlightenment reason

The European Enlightenment is seen as a watershed in the development of modern ideology. By its defenders, the Enlightenment is portrayed as a movement on behalf of reason, justice, freedom and equality — secular ideals that stand in marked contrast to the religious obscurantism, philosophical dogmatism and political absolutism of the Dark Ages. The essential nature of Enlightenment reason can be seen in the work of the German philosopher Immanuel Kant (1724–1804). Kant rejected the idea of absolute value, according to which an idea or a thing is worthy because it has some inherent value or 'goodness'. He insisted that the only factor in determining human action is (or should be) reason, based on universal rules and principles which are (or should be) intelligible to all people. We can summarise this rationalist outlook as follows:

- Reason is based on universal rules: failure to act rationally can be explained as a consequence of failure to act in accordance with abstract reason.
- What is 'right' according to the principles of reason is superior to subjective ideas of the 'good': subjective ideas of the 'goodness' of a thing cannot be used to justify its 'rightness'.
- Reason requires that individuals be impartial rather than show favour towards specific values or beliefs: a rational society is one in which people are objective and cosmopolitan (exposed to numerous cultural influences rather than one dominant view).

Although Kant acknowledged that his rationalist outlook would be more difficult to realise in the private sphere than the public sphere (since most people lack the maturity or courage to be *truly* impartial in their private affairs), his optimistic assessment was received with some scepticism by conservative thinkers, who argued that such a view ignores the complex motives that drive human behaviour. From a conservative perspective, to portray human motives in such a disinterested way is to misunderstand the essence of human nature.

At the centre of conservative thought, therefore, lies a tension between two philosophical schools of thought: rationalism and pragmatism. Rationalists promote a methodical, scientific outlook, a willingness to experiment and a positive attitude towards change, whereas pragmatists emphasise that nothing that is inherently worth having can be invented.

If rationalism implies a commitment to reason, logic and impartiality, then pragmatism implies a corresponding commitment to 'common sense', experience and contingency. In effect, pragmatism is a way of thinking that says that the value of something must be measured by its practical outcome.

Pragmatists are opposed to doctrines such as rationalism, which hold that truth can be arrived at through a process of deduction, arguing instead for a cautious, step-by-step approach to change, based on experience. For the pragmatist, empirical experience is everything: experience allows us to avoid the pitfalls of speculation, by avoiding questions that have no application and no verifiable answers. Since the eighteenth century, the ideas of both rationalism and pragmatism have influenced the development of modern political ideologies such as liberalism, conservatism and socialism.

Rationalism is usually associated with radical change. Liberal rationalists place their faith in science and education, which they see as vehicles of social progress. They embrace rationalist concepts and ideas because these provide the basis for challenging convention and tradition. In the modern age, rationalism has made great progress precisely because it has been tied to the idea of science: rationalist ways of thinking have benefited mankind, improving health and education, reducing poverty, and contributing to the overall advancement of human welfare. Indeed, some liberal rationalists still believe in a 'linear' concept of progress — the idea that the world is advancing towards a higher level of civilisation.

Pragmatism appeals to those of a more conservative disposition. This is because conservatives believe that 'grand theories' and 'rationalist speculation' lead to unpredictable outcomes. Social and political problems can only be dealt with using practical methods adapted to the circumstances in question, rather than by methods that conform to an ideology. For the pragmatic conservative, the guiding principle is not what could be the case in an ideal world, but rather what is the case in this world — here and now. Experience guides the pragmatist to believe that rationalist ways of thinking are risky, ill-considered and utopian in their conception.

If an institution has stood the test of time, it deserves to be defended rather than subjected to constant change and revision. If change is necessary, it should be conducted within the framework of existing methods, and not in accordance with any random ideological scheme.

Oakeshott's critique of rationalism

To its supporters, conservatism offers a *consistent* and a *realistic* vision of politics, society and the individual, and the relations between them. Conservatives call for a 'free and decent' society, with responsible citizens, strong civic organisations and a small but effective government. One of the most important contributions to modern conservative political thought is an essay by the English writer Michael Oakeshott entitled 'Rationalism in politics'. Oakeshott attacks what he calls the rationalist faith in technique. According to Oakeshott, politics is essentially an art rather than science: politicians should be diplomats, balancing interests, identifying alliances and introducing timely reforms in order to preserve rather than transform the institutions of society. The rationalist, argues Oakeshott,

> believes in argument as the technique and operation of 'reason'; the truth of an opinion and the 'rational' ground (not the use) of an institution is all that matters to him. Consequently, much of his political activity consists in bringing the social, political, legal and institutional inheritance of his society before the tribunal of his intellect; and the rest is rational administration, 'reason' exercising an uncontrolled jurisdiction over the circumstances of the case. To the rationalist, nothing is of value merely because it exists (and certainly not because it has existed for many generations), familiarity has no worth, and nothing is to be left standing for want of scrutiny. And his disposition makes both destruction and creation easier for him to understand and engage in, than acceptance or reform.
>
> Michael Oakeshott, 'Rationalism in politics', in
> *Rationalism in Politics and Other Essays* (1947)

For Oakeshott, therefore, the idea of politics as a 'science' is based on a flawed perception that political problems can be resolved through social engineering: such assumptions not only ignore the immense complexity of human social life, but also the unpredictability and fallibility of human nature. Two further problems with rationalism are the politics of perfection and the politics of uniformity.

First, rationalists (particularly liberals and socialists) assume that humanity can be moulded in accordance with some rational design, and that human conduct can be guided and shaped in conformity with an ideal or utopian vision. From a pragmatic conservative perspective, such visions of a utopian or perfect society are forms of social engineering that inevitably increase human suffering by offering people an ideal future that can never be realised in practice.

Second, rationalists also believe in 'uniformity'; that there are universal, uniform solutions that can be applied to all social and political ills. Such ideas can be traced back to the Enlightenment — to the view that difference is something to be overcome, that nature itself can be subjected to the sovereignty of technique, and that everything can ultimately be reduced to an administrative problem.

Oakeshott traced the rationalist belief in perfection and uniformity back to the Enlightenment idea that mankind, having thrown off the shackles of

religion and superstition, had bestowed upon itself the capacity to order the human and natural world at will. This fatal conceit, he argued, is the central problem of politics because the laws guiding human conduct cannot be subject to human will.

Burke's critique of revolution

Like Oakeshott, the eighteenth-century philosopher Edmund Burke (1729–97) was appalled by what he saw as the consequences of rationalism in politics. For Burke, the events of the French Revolution demonstrated the dangers of sudden, dramatic political change: the act of regicide not only destroyed the principle of hereditary monarchy in France, but also threatened the existing political power and social privilege of the aristocracy throughout Europe. Burke appealed to the revolutionaries in Paris to understand the dangers inherent in their zeal to transform France from a legitimate monarchy to a republic based on popular sovereignty. This, he argued, would put power in the hands of those (the 'Third Estate') with the least experience, the least restraint and the least understanding, resulting in chaos and violence:

> Whenever the supreme authority is vested in a body so composed, it must evidently produce the consequences of supreme authority placed in the hands of men not taught habitually to respect themselves; who had no previous fortune in character at stake; who could not be expected to bear with moderation, or to conduct with discretion, a power, which they themselves, more than any others, must be surprised to find in their hands. Who could flatter himself that these men...would not be intoxicated with their unprepared greatness?
>
> Edmund Burke, *Reflections on the Revolution in France* (1790)

Burke emphasised the dangers of mob rule, fearing that the Jacobins' zeal — their desire to reset the calendar itself back to 'year zero' — would destroy French society and set a precedent for future challenges to authority, tradition, hierarchy and property. However, while his observations were an inspiration to counter-revolutionaries, Burke's refusal to acknowledge the anachronistic nature of the *ancien régime*, his lack of sympathy with the revolution and his misunder-standing of the long-term significance of the events of 1789 mean that he is classified less as a cautious pragmatist than as a reactionary.

In modern conservatism, the tensions between pragmatism and rationalism are visible in the distance between traditional and New Right conservatism. This becomes most apparent in the way traditional and New Right conservatives think about the individual and the rights and freedoms of individuals within society. Pragmatists tend to be more cautious about the value of individualism, emphasising identity and obligation to community. Rationalists, on the other hand, support a more libertarian view that the individual should have the freedom and right to decide what is best for him or herself. As we shall see in Chapter 4, there are links between classical liberalism and libertarian New Right thinking, particularly in relation to economic freedom and the role of the state in society. For the New Right, the idea that economic freedom should be curtailed in the interests of social cohesion is rejected in favour of individualism and deregulation.

What are the implications of anti-rationalism for the conservative view of human nature?

It is often assumed that conservatives hold a sceptical or even pessimistic view of human nature, as if human beings in a state of nature are amoral, predatory and asocial creatures who require guidance and discipline. This view rehearses an idea familiar to traditional beliefs that depict mankind in biblical terms as a fallen race, cast out from Eden by a vengeful God dismayed at the cupidity of human beings. But this simplistic interpretation conceals a more complex picture, in which human nature is multilayered and subject to contradictory forces. In order to understand this view, it is first of all necessary to clarify what we mean by 'human nature' and why the issue of human nature plays a central role in ideological thought.

Human nature may be defined as those consistent and invariant attributes and characteristics that make up and define human social, psychological and cultural ways of being, acting and thinking.

The question of human nature lies at the heart of all ideological thinking. All political ideologies say something about:

- what human nature is
- what it is capable of achieving
- its limitations

There are many sources of knowledge about what human nature is, including myths, religion, proverbs, literature, philosophy and science. Increasingly, however, understanding of human nature is based on knowledge obtained through sciences such as biology, medicine and psychology, rather than through superstition or mythology. Social scientists and philosophers are interested in human nature for a variety of reasons, but the main reason for this stems from the belief that *human beings can be improved.*

In the eighteenth century, rationalist thinkers began to suggest that it might be possible to perfect man-made institutions if only we had sufficient knowledge of human nature. Thinkers such as August Comte (1798–1857) believed it would be possible to develop a positive (i.e. definite and unquestionable) 'science of man' — in effect, a psychological and social science of the human mind. Likewise, Henri Saint-Simon (1760–1825) believed that once philosophers and sociologists had discovered how and why people arrive at their beliefs, they could develop rational techniques for promoting a 'correct' form of ideological consciousness.

This kind of rationalist approach was popular among reformist liberals and radical socialists, who came to believe that the human mind is rather like a *tabula rasa*, or blank slate, which, through socialisation and education, can be so constituted as to make the individual more dynamic, more ethical and even more intelligent. Comte's belief can be summarised as follows: if we can discover the right pedagogical (educational) techniques, it will be possible to instil a 'correct' form of consciousness as a basis for the continual evolution of human rationality.

As latter-day rationalists, Marxists in particular reject any idea of human nature as fixed or constant, arguing that human nature is in reality a **historical category** — that the human race consciously reproduces the conditions of its own existence. From this perspective, theories of human nature are ideological expressions that reflect the leading social and political values of the day.

Although some scientists still hold such beliefs today (and genetics offers the possibility of a radical alteration of human nature through the manipulation of DNA), the optimism of the eighteenth century has been tempered by the manifest resistance of human nature to the beneficial effects of 'enlightened reform'. However, there are links between the rise of positive science and the ways in which individuals are initiated into modes of conduct appropriate to the reproduction of authority relations.

This point has been made by the philosopher Michel Foucault (1926–84), who argues that the origins of modern scientific disciplines such as medicine, psychiatry and political economy lie in the desire of authorities to control their populations and maximise their usefulness. As technologies of social control, scientific disciplines allow authorities to act on the mind by acting on the physical body.

Conservative scepticism

From a conservative perspective, the emergence of radical ideologies such as socialism can be traced back to the optimism of eighteenth-century rationalism, which held out the possibility of a radical transformation of human nature.

Whereas liberals advocate the gradual improvement of the human mind, and socialists place their faith in the cultivation of a 'socialist personality', conservatives doubt the capacity of human beings to overcome the economic, psychological and cultural constraints on the development of human reason. In contrast with the deterministic assumptions of some liberals and radical socialists, conservatives reject the view that consciousness can be manipulated through social conditioning to produce ideal human beings. In this sense, conservatives reject the kind of cognitive-developmental theories of psychologists such as Jean Piaget (1896–1980), who identified universal stages in the formation of children's character as they internalise ways of thinking and being.

Jean Piaget, whose theories of child development are rejected by conservatives

However, if conservatives reject deterministic assumptions concerning the 'plasticity' of human nature and its susceptibility to behavioural modification, this does not mean they reject scientific theories of human nature altogether. On the contrary, conservatives stress that human beings are essentially fallible creatures, subject to a range of contradictory drives and motives.

The conservative view can be summarised as follows. First, human nature is complex: individuals are capable of rational thought and moral action, but can also be wilfully ignorant, callous and despicable towards their fellows and their natural environment. This basic instability renders human nature fallible, for even though we may be perfectly aware that a more rational or moral form of action is possible, we often still choose to act in a selfish, stupid or evil way.

Second, individuals are security-seeking creatures, who must satisfy their basic physical and emotional needs before they are capable of higher-level moral

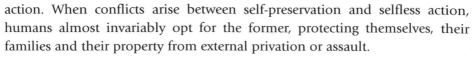

action. When conflicts arise between self-preservation and selfless action, humans almost invariably opt for the former, protecting themselves, their families and their property from external privation or assault.

Third, humans crave identity and a sense of 'connectedness'. The potential boundlessness of human existence (the fact that there are so many choices available to us) makes it necessary to impose some form of order on human conduct. Traditional institutions such as heterosexual marriage, the family, organised religion and private property are seen as invaluable because they give stability and structure to people's lives, impose social control and foster respect for authority.

In summary, therefore, conservatives stress — in a more or less consistent way — the non-perfectibility of human nature rather than the continual evolution of human rationality. Although this view contains an element of scepticism about the capacity of humankind to create an ideal world, the pragmatic emphasis in conservative thought is oriented towards defence of traditions and practices over those which may be externally induced. There are, as we shall see in subsequent chapters, some differences between the way traditional and modern conservatives see human nature, but it is possible to conclude that conservatism is based on a consistent ideological view of the potential of human beings to transcend the natural limitations of their biological inheritance.

A traditional church wedding

The ideological essence of conservatism

Those who see conservatism more as a disposition argue that the conservative outlook is essentially a pragmatic one, defined in contrast to the rationalistic outlook of Enlightenment thinkers such as Kant. Those who emphasise the more ideological dimension of conservatism, on the other hand, suggest that there are indeed systematic elements in conservative thought that cannot be reduced to a question of temperament.

From the analysis in the preceding section, however, it should be clear that conservatism entails a particular view of human nature, so in this respect at least it can be seen as an ideological form of thought. Although earlier forms of political conservatism were more closely linked to an everyday preference for the conventional and the familiar, political conservatism is as much an ideology as liberalism, socialism, feminism and anarchism. The argument that it is nothing more than a pragmatic outlook ignores the important functions of conservative ideology for those who identify with or hold conservative values and beliefs.

One of the most insightful observers of conservatism was the sociologist Karl Mannheim (1893–1947). Mannheim examined the origins and development of conservatism in Germany in the nineteenth century, which he compared with the evolution of English Toryism, and concluded that the central problem for conservatives is *how to manage change*. According to Mannheim, conservatism 'crystallises out of the psychological attitude of traditionalism among social actors who experience these developments as harmful, but cannot ignore them or simply respond in private, individual ways' (Mannheim, 'Introduction' to *Conservatism*, 1986).

In this sense, political conservatism is an ideological formulation based on a romantic attachment to traditional ways of life. However, as this conservative disposition became more systematic and self-conscious, it came to resemble more closely the liberal rationalism that it opposes. The proof of this can be seen in the development of political conservatism since the nineteenth century.

The functions of ideologies

The key point to consider is that ideologies fulfil a specific set of functions: namely, mobilisation, legitimation and representation.

Mobilisation

Ideologies mobilise individuals and groups behind political goals. Mobilisation is a positive function of ideology because political action requires commitment and participation from those involved. Without ideology, groups lack a clear political profile, and one of the basic functions of ideology is to codify and emphasise core concepts and values while excluding alternative concepts and values that may conflict with these. Although conservatives rarely engage in political activism, they employ established forms of political organisation to mobilise their supporters. A good example of this is the Christian Coalition in the USA in the 1990s, which mobilised its supporters against liberal welfarism. Such grassroots campaigns succeed by mobilising positive identification with a core ideological message.

Legitimation

Ideologies also serve to legitimate economic and social interests. Ruling-class ideologies, in particular, tend to favour those interests that are supportive of the system, and marginalise those that seek to change the status quo. Unlike anarchism, for example, which seeks to transform social reality in accordance with a utopian vision of the ideal society, conservatism is essentially a 'system-functional' ideology that allows rulers to justify their policies in terms of prevailing values and beliefs. In this sense, conservatism serves to sustain a particular type of class society by presenting its values and beliefs as timeless and universal rather than temporary and sectional.

Representation

Political ideologies specify a particular way of representing social reality, and help to translate vague ideas and beliefs into concrete goals. As such, they 'give shape' to everyday experience and reinforce collective identities. Although less explicitly doctrinal in form than anarchism or Marxism, conservatism represents social reality in such a way as to help individuals and groups to pursue their goals. Traditional forms of conservatism are clearly more pragmatic in their defence of customs and convention, while modern New Right conservatism is more assertive of individualism and economic freedom.

Shifting values

In the early nineteenth century, the main thrust of conservative politics was defensive and reactive, designed to arrest the advance of new social forces brought into existence by industrialisation. A good example of this phenomenon is early conservative opposition to free trade, which was seen as potentially harmful to aristocratic landowning interests. By the second half of the nineteenth century, however, conservatives had abandoned their commitment to protectionism, although it was not until the 1970s that the Conservative Party in the UK fully embraced the idea of free trade as an alternative to managed capitalism. With the ascent of Thatcherism, conservative ideology shifted sharply towards an explicit defence of the market.

Critics of conservatism often argue that this shift in values is indicative of the opportunistic nature of conservatism, which survives by adapting to prevailing ideological reality. As Marxist commentators argue, however, the point of an ideology is to legitimise a system of social relations by promoting positive identification among social groups whose real interests might be served better by adopting a more critical outlook. The difference between traditional and modern conservatism is determined largely by the different economic and social interests of privileged groups in society, whose primary aim is to protect their wealth and social status against the encroachments of other groups.

- **Paternalistic conservatism** emerged in the nineteenth century as an elitist ideology based on the assumption that ruling elites have both a right and a duty to govern by virtue of their superior birth, knowledge and status.
- **New Right conservatism**, on the other hand, is a populist ideology designed to broaden the appeal of capitalism by extending private ownership, choice and consumerism. The advance of the New Right in the 1980s occurred by extending the appeal of market capitalism among lower middle-class and working-class voters disillusioned with traditional socialism.

The appeal of conservatism

There is little question that conservatism is a distinctive political doctrine — one which is more radical than its supporters might wish to admit. However, the appeal of conservatism at the instinctive level is also very strong, particularly if we acknowledge the close affinity between right-wing ideologies and national–popular sentiment.

In the 1980s, for example, the Conservatives in the UK portrayed themselves as the party committed to a return to 'Victorian values' — a vague but nevertheless effective slogan that was designed to evoke the virtues of a bygone age. This tendency was documented by Mannheim, who observed that 'Conservative thinking raises older ways of thinking and behaving to the level of reflection and thereby rescues them from being buried, but simultaneously creates a new fruitful way of thinking' (Mannheim 1986).

Yet beneath the rhetoric of the Victorian virtues of perseverance, patriotism and thrift lay a deep commitment to the ideology of laissez-faire capitalism. This provided a firm ideological basis for the political–economic adjustments of the Thatcher period, which had a radical effect on UK society in the 1980s and 1990s.

It would be a mistake, therefore, to ignore the radicalism in some forms of conservative thought. Conservatives are indeed traditionalists who prefer 'common sense' ways of thinking and acting to abstract theorising; but to insist that conservatism is *only* a form of conventionalism is to ignore the many changes that conservative political parties have introduced in the nineteenth and twentieth centuries. To reduce conservatism to traditionalism would also be to overlook the fact that traditions themselves are expressions of embedded interests: customs and conventions (including the idea of 'common sense' pragmatism) can be seen as manifestations of the aspirations of social groups. By defending hegemonic values, customs and traditions, which are seen as essential to the preservation of the existing structure of hierarchy and privilege

in society, conservatives legitimise social practices, at an ideological level, which are supportive of their interests.

Paternalistic and New Right conservatism

However, it is important to reaffirm the ideological distinction between paternalistic and New Right conservatism. There is evidence to suggest that New Right ideology is more open to the concept of a naturally evolving human rationality, and therefore less inclined towards a cautious pragmatism.

A key intellectual source of this current of thought was the philosopher Friedrich Hayek (1899–1992), whose liberal conservatism is based on the assumption that social order should be naturally evolving rather than guided by the state. As an economic liberal with an ambivalent attitude towards authority, Hayek's outlook represents an important crossover point between liberalism and conservatism, which share a basic interest in economic freedom as a precondition for the survival of capitalist society.

As we shall see in Chapter 5, however, Hayek's libertarian reasoning pays little attention to the economic coercion used to control human conduct in liberal-capitalist societies. In contrast to older forms of political coercion, economic coercion creates strong incentives for conformism and respect for authority by linking prosperity and status to personal achievement within a competitive system of exchange.

Conclusion

It is clear, therefore, that, while conservatism was born of a traditionalist outlook in the nineteenth century, the emergence of conservatism as a political doctrine reflects a distinctive, consciously cultivated, systematic worldview. Since the nineteenth century, conservatism has developed into a set of political ideologies oriented towards the defence of existing ways of life and existing patterns of privilege, and in opposition to progressive or utopian political ideologies such as liberalism, socialism and anarchism.

During the twentieth century, however, conservatism absorbed and adapted influences from other ideologies — most notably, Manchester liberalism. Partly for this reason, modern conservatism represents a more explicit defence of private economic interests, seemingly at odds with the 'organic' theory of society advanced by early conservative theorists. Yet despite this shift in emphasis, there remains a core set of intuitive ideological values within conservative thought, most important among these being a rigorous defence of authority and tradition. Conservatism cannot be reduced to a question of temperament, for to do so risks equating what is a clearly defined political doctrine with simple traditionalism, which is itself nothing more than a general state of mind based on a stubborn attachment to old ways of life and fear of innovation.

Task 1.1

Read Source A and complete the questions that follow.

Source A

There is indeed a compatibility between conservative ideology and some expressions of religious belief. The inherent weakness and wickedness of man has been proclaimed by Christian thinkers down the ages; man is incapable of redeeming himself [sic] through his own efforts. Therefore, ideologies such

5 as liberalism, socialism and, most especially, anarchism, which present an optimistic picture of human nature and human potentiality, are at odds with the mainstream orthodox Christian faith, which suggests that Christ's intercession is necessary for human salvation. And, just as human beings are too inherently flawed to achieve everlasting salvation through their own unaided

10 efforts, so these same weaknesses prevent spontaneous cooperative endeavour, and require authority and strong government to keep men in order

Robert Leach, *Political Ideology in Britain* (2002)

(a) Why have conservative thinkers focused on the 'weakness and wickedness' of mankind (line 2)?

(b) Why do conservatives doubt the capacity of mankind to achieve 'salvation' without divine intercession (lines 4–8)?

(c) If human imperfection and weakness of character 'prevent spontaneous cooperative endeavour' (line 10), what does this say about the possibility of socialism or anarchism?

Guidance

Conservatives, as we have seen, have a sceptical view of human nature. They see humankind as having a higher, more advanced level of understanding and a lower, base nature. The latter is more resistant to moral guidance, hence the need for authority and other forms of social control. Without such control, individuals will have less incentive to act responsibly, and will be unable to control their drive to dominate their fellows or harm their rivals.

Conservatives doubt that humans are capable of rational self-organisation, which makes it extremely unlikely that well-meaning people could form stateless cooperative communities (as anarchists and others recommend). Guidance and authority must therefore come from above, either from God or from the institutions of state and society, without which — as Thomas Hobbes argued — society risks descending into a chaos of competing wills.

Chapter 1

Task 1.2

Copy and complete the following table.

Ideology	Key thinkers	Perspective on human nature
Liberalism		
Socialism		
Conservatism		
Anarchism		
Fascism		

Guidance

Try to establish how thinkers within each tradition have approached the problem of human nature, and what human nature is capable of. Liberals are realistic about the potential corruptibility of human beings, but remain optimistic about the possibility of human progress. Why?

Fascist ideologists take an extreme position, doubting the capacity of uncultured or 'inferior' individuals to make reasoned decisions without reference to authority. How does this compare with conservatism, or indeed collectivist anarchism?

Remember that the key to understanding conservatism is to link conservatives' idea of human imperfection with a pragmatic defence of authority and social control. This idea is notably lacking in socialism and anarchism, but is a key feature of fascism.

Useful websites

- For two views of conservative theories of human nature, see:
  www.kirkcenter.org/kirk/ten-principles.html
  http://www.conservatoroccidentalis.com/?p=15
- For a more radical secular conservative account of human nature, see:
  http://rightreason.ektopos.com/archives/2005/10/the_conservativ.html

Further reading

- Burke, E. (1790) *Reflections on the Revolution in France*, 1999 edn, Oxford University Press.
- Mannheim, K. (1986) *Conservatism*, Routledge & Kegan Paul.
- Oakeshott, M. (1947) 'Rationalism in politics', in *Rationalism in Politics and Other Essays*, 1991 edn, Liberty Fund.

Why do conservatives value authority and tradition?

Introduction

Two of the most important components of conservative ideology are respect for authority and defence of tradition. In this chapter, we will attempt to understand why these are such important values for conservatives, and why these values above all else serve to differentiate conservative theories from liberal and socialist theories of society.

Conservatives have a strong preference for traditional forms of authority that have their basis in institutions such as the family, the Church, the law, the police and other 'authority-bearing' social structures. Conservatives argue that there is a close link between declining respect for authority in modern societies and rising levels of criminality and social disorder. Unlike liberals and socialists, they maintain that defence of authority is a basic condition for the defence of liberty, for without respect for law and order, society is at risk of disintegration. In return, liberals and socialists suggest that reliance on authority to sustain a structure of social relations can be problematic, particularly if an established structure is challenged, provoking an authoritarian response from those in positions of social control.

In many respects, authority and tradition are mutually reinforcing: respect for custom and tradition helps to sustain authority, while authority helps to preserve customary and traditional ways of life. Few social organisations can function without some kind of authority, and even anarchists concede that authority can resolve coordination problems.

What is authority?

There is a distinction between power and authority, which must be grasped if we are to understand the specific value of authority for conservatives. In its simplest sense, power is the ability to do something or to make something happen — the capacity to act upon a person or thing and determine an outcome.

Authority is best defined as a form of normative guidance, a means of exerting control by encouraging individuals to see that their own interests are also served through compliance with the authoritative commands of superiors. As Joseph Raz (1990) argues, 'the special problem with authority is not that it requires one regard the will of another as one's reason for action, but that it requires one to let authoritative directives pre-empt one's own judgement. One should comply with them whether or not one agrees with them'. In other words, acceptance of authority is based on unquestioning obedience.

In political terms, authority is defined as: the *right to enforce obedience or to make an ultimate decision*. For a political system to function without resort to coercion, power must be exercised in a legitimate way by government. It must, in other words, take the form of authority. Although power can be exercised without legitimacy, authority requires a positive moral justification, indicating not simply a capacity to issue commands but a *right* to govern.

Max Weber (1864–1920) famously defined three ideal types of authority, which he termed 'legitimate rulership'. These are traditional, charismatic and legal–rational authority:

- **Traditional authority** is the kind possessed by kings and feudal lords over their subjects. Although less evident in modern society, traditional authority is still relevant in some spheres: for example, the authority of a headmaster over the staff and pupils in an old-fashioned public school.
- **Charismatic authority** is based on the qualities of individuals as figures of authority. The word 'charisma' comes from the ancient Greek word for 'gift', implying that the individual on whom authority is bestowed is in possession of an unusual form of power over others.
- **Legal–rational authority** is the most prevalent in modern societies that are based on bureaucratic systems of government and the rule of law. Weber argued that legal–rational authority is based not on individuals but on office holders: that is, people have authority not because of who they are but because of their position or function within organisations.

Weber acknowledged that, in the real world, authority rarely conforms exactly to one pure type or another, and may be based on a mixture of sources.

For example, charismatic authority tends to increase the legitimacy of governments by allowing subjects to identify with a dynamic leader. This was certainly the case in the Soviet Union under Stalin, as well as in Iraq under Saddam Hussein.

On what grounds do conservatives support authority?

The key point for conservatives is that authority — and political authority in particular — is a vital resource for a stable and prosperous society. Conservatives recognise that governments must, in the final analysis, rely on coercive power to back up their decisions (if they don't, they will fall). But they insist that authority *augments* (adds to) the power of superiors by encouraging citizens to believe that their commands are rightful. Without this belief — however unfounded — societies lack a basic source of integration and good government becomes more difficult to sustain.

Political authority

In political theory, authority is usually divided into its *de facto* and *de jure* forms. Where authority is recognised and accepted, we define it as *de facto* authority. An individual or an institution either has *de facto* authority or it does not. The source of such authority may be unclear, but subjects nevertheless comply. Where authority is justified, we call it *de jure* authority.

Under normal conditions, *de facto* and *de jure* authority coincide: an authority which is effective may not require formal legitimisation (because people already accept its right to issue commands); but where authority is *also* legal and justified, it is more likely to be effective and binding without resort to coercion, even under difficult circumstances. A legally justified authority is always more stable and more effective precisely because it is justified in terms of the values and beliefs of the ruled.

In this sense, the *authority of rulers is only really justified if it is effective.* Governments possess authority because they claim a right to rule and succeed in establishing a legitimate claim to rule. A political authority may not be owed a duty of obedience if it acts outside the law, but there is no such thing as a political authority that does not claim a duty of obedience, for all claims to authority are based on this assumption. However, for conservatives, authority is important not just in politics but in social life generally. Authorities regulate human behaviour in various areas of life, but in an ideal sense, authority as a general resource helps to condition human conduct without the need for direct coercion.

Why should individuals obey authority?

An important question remains: why should individuals obey authority? Obligation to obey authority is usually justified on three main grounds.

Voluntarist theories

According to followers of John Locke (1632–1704), authority is justified only if it is grounded on the consent of citizens. Although few people actually do consent to be governed, residence within a state and participation in elections are often taken to be expressions of approval. More recent philosophers such as H. L. A. Hart (1907–92) and John Rawls (1921–2002) have developed this approach using the idea of 'fair play', according to which participation in a cooperative scheme means that we have a natural duty to obey the law. If a person benefits from living in a just system, and plans to continue benefiting from that system, then he or she has a duty to obey its rules.

Communitarian theories

Some philosophers believe that, in the absence of an actual contract between rulers and ruled, the only basis for political authority lies in associative obligations. Philosophers such as Michael Sandel (1953–) stress that we have obligations to obey the law because this is part of what it means to be members of communities. This view is based on the idea that who we are in our social contexts tells us what kind of obligations we have. This is not a voluntary situation; it is a consequence of being born into and resident within a specific cultural-linguistic group.

Utilitarian theories

A third type of justification is based on utilitarianism, which holds that individuals should respect authority and obey the law because such conduct will increase the welfare of the community as a whole. Utilitarian philosophers use the 'generalisation argument' to make this point: what would happen if everyone broke the law? Clearly, law-abiding individuals stand to gain more by agreeing to be bound by the requirements of authority, which enables society to coordinate social action for the benefit of all citizens.

Political authority and the strands of conservatism

At first glance there would seem to be an intuitive link between the conservative view of authority and the communitarian justification for authority. However, it would be wrong to ignore the influence of other ideological traditions on the way conservatives understand authority, and a distinction must be drawn between the way authoritarian, libertarian and paternalistic conservatives interpret the proper function of authority and control in society.

Authoritarian conservatives

Authoritarian conservatives favour hierarchy and authority as pillars of social order, and social scientists have attempted to link this preference to a particular personality type. A well-known US study of the authoritarian personality (Adorno et al. 1950) identified a personality pattern based on the desire for order, security, power and hierarchy, combined with a need for clear lines of authority, a preference for conventional values, a demand for unquestioning obedience, and a hostility towards outsiders. Individuals who conform to this personality type feel comfortable in hierarchical organisations that release the individual from responsibility to make autonomous decisions.

In ideological terms, however, authoritarian conservatism tends to disguise a reactionary social and political agenda by using authority to prevent the growth and development of emancipatory social movements. In an attempt to defend the established structure of power and privilege and to control patterns of modernisation, reactionary governments employ authoritarian measures to restrict the growth of pluralism and democracy. This results in a form of 'rule from above', in which traditional elites (the landowning class, the officer corps, the Church etc.) combine to resist pressures for change.

At best, authoritarian rule results in limited suppression of freedoms (e.g. suspension of civil liberties, reduction of press freedom and prohibition of strikes), and a system of guided democracy in which elites retain control over key positions of state. At worst, it results in the repression of civil society by the armed organs of

Reuters/Rickey Rogers

Chilean dictator, Pinochet, reviewing his troops

the state, as occurred in Latin America in the 1970s. Such regimes are, however, rarely stable, due to a lack of legitimacy. The insulation of the leadership from criticism leads to a delusion of infallibility and a failure to integrate strategic groups into positions of influence.

Paternalistic conservatives

Paternalistic conservatives adopt a middle-way approach to authority, according to which both state and non-state institutions have a role to play in normative (morally binding) guidance. Paternalists believe in the importance of deference to authority, which succeeds by excluding private judgement: authoritative reasons do not simply outweigh competing criteria; rather, they exclude alternative factors as irrelevant, inducing subjects to 'surrender' their own private judgement in the face of binding commands. Ideologically, paternalistic conservatives recognise the importance of authority for determining goals and providing moral leadership. For paternalistic conservatives, authority is a prior condition for liberty. Without respect for authority and the rule of law, social organisation is impossible.

In the nineteenth century, English conservatives were committed to a conception of authority and the 'general good' that entrusted authority to the ruling class. Over time, however, this vision of aristocratic leadership became redundant when confronted by the growing power of the executive branch of the state. The response of Tory traditionalists was to oppose further democratisation in the hope of holding back democratic change. For realists, however, the most sensible response lay in challenging the Liberals and the emergent Labour Party for control of the executive in order to exert a greater level of influence over the future extension of state authority into different spheres of society.

Libertarian conservatives

Libertarian conservatives take a very different approach to authority. It is suggested by some philosophers that the libertarian preference for personal freedom, choice and autonomy contradicts the very idea of authority: if person A exercises authority over person B, then a relation of power is created whereby B forfeits the right to moral self-direction. However, the libertarian conservative view of authority and liberty is more subtle and complex than this simple scenario allows.

The principal target of libertarian ideology is not authority as such, but the extended authority of organised systems of power in modern societies — specifically, but not exclusively, the sovereign power of the modern state. The libertarian conservative understanding of virtue entails a return to a natural order, based on the sovereign individual and voluntaristic community. This libertarian ideal emphasises the view that true virtue derives from the development of

'organic institutions' and authority structures within civil society rather than from the organised authority of the centralised state. For libertarian conservatives, the key sites of authority are the family, community organisations and other forms of civil association, which allow for the decentralisation of power and the preservation of local autonomy.

Summary

Contrary to familiar stereotypes, therefore, the conservative view of authority is in fact complex. On the one hand, there is the familiar attack on permissive liberal values, which conservatives hold responsible for undermining the moral fabric of society. On the other hand, however, there is an attack on the centralising power of the state, which libertarian conservatives hold responsible for the demise of local forms of authority and social control.

In conclusion, it seems that the conservative outlook is most powerful in its defence of traditional forms of authority. Libertarian and paternalistic conservatives disagree about the need for state management and state control, but there is a basic agreement that the activities of the state should be subordinate to the needs of society rather than vice versa. Respect for and deference to authority are understood to be positive phenomena, reflecting an underlying faith in the value of normative guidance, i.e. where the conduct of individuals is guided by the appropriate norms, moral values and conventions of social life.

Without normative guidance, society risks descending into uncontrolled individualism and non-conformism, with negative consequences for social order. If, on the other hand, individuals 'know their place' and are able to exercise self-discipline, then society can be regulated in a 'natural' way, without the need for a coercive state. Conservatives believe that the moral decline of modern western societies lies precisely in the collapse of respect for authority. They blame this collapse on the 'trendy' social theories of liberals and socialists, who reject the assumption that authority should be instilled in the young and favour a more progressive approach.

Why do conservatives value tradition?

Although there are important differences in the way conservative traditionalists and conservative modernisers view tradition, defence of tradition is — like respect for authority — a core component of conservative ideologies. As Burke noted, the very possibility of society is conditional upon on the maintenance of a contract between generations: each generation has a duty to learn from experience, to honour the achievements and sacrifices of its ancestors, and to preserve these for future generations. In practical terms, this means that conservatives have a natural preference for tried-and-tested methods, but will usually be unafraid to abandon these if they do not serve their political purposes.

Rules, customs and conventions

Rules, customs and conventions strengthen social integration by binding individuals to certain forms of conduct and ways of life. Conservative philosophers argue that following rules is less a conscious process (i.e. one in which we deduce what we should do from a list of instructions) than an unconscious one based on experience and repetition. As members of communities, we are socialised to understand the 'rules of the game' through a process of demonstration and training, where rational explanations are largely absent. This allows us to see what is expected of us without lengthy reasoning or questioning, and prepares us for the many and varied demands made on us throughout our lives.

Rules and conventions also serve to maintain a sense of common identity and common purpose by defining what is expected of us in our different social roles. In this way, rules and conventions promote a sense of 'rootedness' or 'connectedness', an innate sense of belonging in a specific place and time. As the anthropologist Arnold Gehlen (1904–76) argued, they help to reduce the complexity of everyday life, which presents individuals with a confusing array of possibilities and choices. In his view, human beings are only able to make sense of reality by selectively creating and following customary ways of being and acting in the world. Without this 'disemburdenment', life in modern civilisation would simply be too overwhelming.

The best way to understand this attachment to tradition is to consider an example of a custom or convention, the existence of which serves to orient individuals to their environment.

One such example is the routine conventions of the working day. Everybody — with the exception of the very rich and the very young — must deal with the idea of routine in their daily lives. From the rituals of getting up in the morning, to the convention of not speaking to complete strangers on the train, to the tradition of sharing a mid-morning coffee break — we all observe habitual practices that help to ease our way in the world and simplify human interaction.

We notice when people break with accepted conventions — particularly if their conduct is offensive — and we become agitated or even anxious if our customary ways of being and acting are seriously threatened. Among conservatives, the appeal of convention and tradition is stronger than it is for liberals, making it more difficult for conservatives — particularly traditional conservatives — to accept change for its own sake.

Tradition

Just as all human social life is governed by conventions, so all societies possess traditions, which are viewed as essential to the self-image of the group. Although the meaning of the term 'tradition' is ambiguous, in the simplest sense it refers to those beliefs, institutions and social practices that have been handed down from one generation to the next: we do things in certain ways because that's how they have always been done. Not to do so would represent a break with the past, possibly undermining the continuity of the community in question.

The expectations generated through common observance of tradition constitute what Roger Scruton (1980) calls social knowledge. Such knowledge is, he argues, the product of convention rather than invention, arising '"by an invisible hand" from the open-ended business of society, from problems which have been confronted and solved, from agreements which have been perpetuated by custom'. This is, however, too simplistic: it tells us very little about:

- the origins of traditions
- the role traditions play in the regulation of contemporary societies

All traditions emerge at some point in history, evolving through a process of adaptation and mutation, drawing on earlier customs and beliefs. Traditions are, in effect, produced and sustained by the societies that observe them, and come into existence as a means for integrating communities within a collective identity. All societies have traditional ways of doing things, but the existence of such traditions cannot be isolated from the social conditions that bring them into being.

A more sophisticated way to think about tradition is to acknowledge that the 'inherited wisdom of the past' is a complex phenomenon constructed through a dialogue between the present and the past. More often than not, traditions come into being through a selective appropriation of relevant ideas and facts that — over time — combine to become binding reasons for action. This idea is expressed by the political theorist Michael Freeden (1996), who points out that concrete traditions represent 'fragmented series of highlighted periods and unexplored places that ideologies cement together'.

Customs and conventions become traditions not just because they represent historically legitimate ways of acting and being, but also because they are deemed relevant to the welfare and collective identity of a given community. Whether or not they are beneficial for the community as a whole, they achieve an unquestioned status in everyday life.

To summarise this point, traditions become conventional ways of doing things because they are, and continue to be, observed by a significant majority of the community. They achieve this status because enough people accept or believe that they matter to give them a kind of 'transcendental' status. As soon as they cease to matter in any real sense, they quickly decline to the status of antiquated custom or ritual.

Consider the example of colonialism. For most British people, the celebration of 'Empire Day' lives on only as a vague memory. Yet only two generations ago it was perfectly acceptable for teachers and community leaders to celebrate the glories of the British empire without reference to the negative impact of colonial rule on African and Asian peoples. In the contemporary UK, the justification of imperialism as a 'civilising mission' is morally unacceptable: it is

War veterans pay their respects to those who fell in the service of their country

no longer possible for Europeans to justify imperialism in this way, and the tradition of glorifying colonialism is now the preserve of a small minority. Other traditions, on the other hand, such as observing 2 minutes' silence on Remembrance Sunday, are maintained because a significant number of British people consider it appropriate to honour the wartime dead — although even this tradition is becoming less prevalent as memories of the two world wars fade in the popular imagination.

How do New Right conservatives differ in their view of tradition?

The principal function of tradition for conservatives is, therefore, its integrating, stabilising effect. Like authority, traditions bind human beings to particular 'norms', which place expectations on social conduct. Customs and cultural practices also serve to mark out the identity of the group, and participation in such normative practices is part of what it means to belong to a given community. If humans deviate at random from such ways of being, this can cause confusion and anxiety — although departure from conventional ways of being is both inevitable and essential for the progress of human civilisation.

Neoliberal conservatives

As might be expected, neoliberal New Right ideologists do not share the unequivocal preference of their neoconservative colleagues for authority and tradition. The neoliberal current running through New Right ideology suggests a different approach to tradition, based on a more rationalist belief in economic freedom and choice.

This approach involves a qualified acceptance of the Enlightenment view of the subject as a calculating, power-seeking individual, but seeks to reconcile this with a concept of authority in which the state is empowered to deal firmly with those who offend against the community.

For neoliberal New Right theorists, the old-fashioned conservative belief in tradition as a source of normative guidance is viewed as anachronistic. New Right conservatives argue that traditional conservatives tend to adapt innovations to suit old purposes. In other words, rather than deal with the source of a problem (such as economic decline), traditionalists prefer to placate their opponents with limited changes designed to preserve social stability.

Libertarian New Right conservatives are more concerned with the deregulation of economic activity than with the preservation of tradition *for its own sake*. They assume that the market can exert an objective form of discipline on individuals, who must work in order to survive.

Their emphasis is on the free market as the guarantor of social stability and on defending the freedom of individuals to make relevant choices for themselves. Traditions have a role to play in sustaining particular forms of culture and identity (to which all conservatives are committed); but traditional forms of regulation — such as the postwar social-democratic consensus — are seen as unconducive to economic growth and prosperity.

Neoconservatives

By contrast, neoconservative New Right thinkers adopt a different approach. Although they support the free market as a mechanism for allocating resources, neoconservatives argue that freedom of choice in economic life must be balanced against the need for authority and social order. Neoconservative thinkers such as Daniel Bell (1919–) focus on the rapid erosion of authority in western society from the 1960s onwards. Bell suggests that the decline of personal responsibility and respect for authority in the West could eventually undermine the work ethic necessary to sustain the dynamism of the capitalist system, and that western societies are in need of moral renewal.

Neoconservatives thus advocate a return to the virtues of diligence, religiosity and the traditional structure of the nuclear family as a way of reinvigorating the moral foundations of capitalist societies. This view has much in common with communitarian theories of society, which aim to balance the excesses of individualism by reasserting a sense of duty, obligation and communal identity. It is clear, however, that an underlying tension exists within New Right ideology, as neoliberal policies frequently unleash social forces that neoconservatives seek to contain. This is apparent in the uncritical commitment of neoliberal New Right conservatives to individualism and the unlimited pursuit of self-interest — values that neoconservatives identify as a reason for the breakdown of social cohesion.

To combat this, neoconservatives emphasise the need for authoritarian measures to deal with the social pressures unleashed by the operation of market forces. This approach can be seen clearly in the case of Conservative law and order policy in the 1990s, which was designed to combat the rise in juvenile delinquency and the increasing incidence of property-related crimes.

Emphasising the importance of authority and respect for law and order, Conservative home secretary Michael Howard justified the government's law and order strategy with the slogan 'prison works'. This policy was designed to reassure anxious voters that tough sentencing policies would deter future criminals, making the streets safer for law-abiding citizens. In ideological terms, this tactic appealed to voters frustrated by the apparent erosion of respect for authority in society, and the failure of 'softly-softly' left-wing approaches to crime and deviance. Michael Howard successfully tapped into a popular feeling that old-fashioned solutions are more effective. However, the Tories made little attempt to link rising crime rates with increasing individualism, social inequality and the breakdown of traditional family and community structures.

Ignoring liberal concerns about the long-term dangers of prison overcrowding, the Conservative 'prison works' campaign concealed an implicit message: namely, that the unpleasantnesses of prison itself should serve as a deterrent for those who might choose to break the law. According to conservatives, this places the onus on the individual to consider the implications of offending against the community, rather than encouraging individuals to believe that they can 'get away with it'. This in turn serves to reinforce the authoritarian–populist view that imprisonment, rather than prevention or rehabilitation, is the only real solution to rising criminality.

H. M. Prison, Manchester, formerly Strangeways

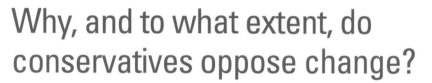

Why, and to what extent, do conservatives oppose change?

In Chapter 1 it was concluded that the central problem for conservatives is how to manage change. From the early nineteenth century onwards, conservatives have drawn a distinction between timely reform and unnecessary change, and Edmund Burke famously argued that 'change is only necessary in order to conserve'.

A natural order

At the heart of conservatism is a preference for evolutionary change as the normal accumulation of history, undistorted by radical experiments in social engineering. Conservatives believe in the idea of an enduring moral order — an order that is 'made' for man, and which man is in turn made to serve. In this sense, human nature is invariant, and moral truths are defined as permanent and resistant to arbitrary adjustment. This style of thinking is unappealing to liberals because it appears to rule out the possibility of 'improvement' through rational reform. It is also unappealing to socialists, as it appears to exclude the possibility of transforming the material basis of human social life.

The essence of the conservative view is that the *moral order within which humans exist is timeless and evolutionary*. This means that there is a kind of 'natural order' which permanently pervades and sustains the universe, but which is essentially *beyond human control*: humans have the ability to act on and alter the conditions of their existence, but are powerless to recreate the natural order to suit their own design. This ideological perspective raises a number of issues.

Changing human values

The assumption of an absolute natural moral order that transcends the spatial and temporal reality of human existence is questionable. There is evidence to suggest that a relationship exists between the substance of human values and beliefs and their social and historical context. Before the emergence of Christianity, for example, most Europeans believed in a pantheistic cosmos (i.e. that there were many different gods). Christian ideas about the value of human life simply did not exist. Likewise, since the Enlightenment, Christianity itself has gone into decline. The development of modern science has discredited spiritual explanations of life and the universe, leading to profound changes in human moral psychology. Although many Christian fundamentalists continue to believe in a revised form of Creationism (now renamed the theory of 'Intelligent Design'), the widely accepted biological theory that humans evolved from cruder life-forms has greatly undermined the authority of Judeo-Christian teachings.

Adapting to change

A second difficulty with the conservative view is that adapting to change is an inevitable part of the human condition. Throughout history, human communities have had to adapt to continual changes in their natural environment (changes in climate, geography etc.) and in their economic way of life. Although the greatest flourishing of human civilisation appears to coincide with extended periods of stability and prosperity, adapting to change is a central facet of human experience.

Conservative radicalism

A third and more difficult problem with the conservative view is that by ruling out fundamental change, conservative thinkers contradict their own political–ideological development. Not only are there numerous instances where conservative politicians have embraced radical change, but there is also plenty of evidence that conservatism can be more radical than its ideological opponents. This is apparent if we examine the changes introduced by UK Conservatives in the 1980s, which radically altered the structure of the economy in favour of private business. By accepting the need for timely change, conservatives have shown themselves to be sufficiently pragmatic to make a virtue of necessity.

Conservatives and social and economic change

Human societies can never be static, and one of the most important criticisms of postwar social theory was its failure to incorporate an adequate historical dimension. By attempting to explain social change in terms of deviation from the norm, conservative sociologists such as Talcott Parsons (1902–79) failed to appreciate the ways in which society evolves through conflict and competitive exchange. By definition, however, conservatives believe in the preservation of existing social arrangements, particularly where these benefit privileged groups. They also favour preserving those moral values, customs and beliefs that are supportive of the system in its present form. Such values, customs and beliefs are not naturally ordained, but in the passage of time assume a hegemonic, 'taken for granted' status that lends them an aura of authority and permanence.

Conservatives do not simply oppose change because all change is negative. Some changes in society are clearly unavoidable (for example, urbanisation is an inevitable consequence of industrialisation), and it is impossible to see how humans could have arrived at their present stage of development without embracing change as a positive feature of human life. The underlying problem for conservatives is not how to avoid change, but *how to reconcile social and*

economic change with the established structure of society. In this sense, there is a strongly pragmatic dimension to the conservative attitude to change. Rather than tamper with the fabric of society by introducing unnecessary changes, the purpose of reform is to increase the legitimacy and stability of the system as a whole. Timely reform is preferable to root-and-branch change, although modern conservatives have shown themselves more willing to accept the need for wholesale reform if it is deemed necessary.

Although conservative thinkers such as Scruton emphasise the importance of convention in the moral and institutional fabric of human communities, defence of tradition and fear of change among conservative politicians is not always consistent. Indeed, it would be absurd for any politician — right-wing or left-wing — to be 'against' change as a matter of course.

Political change under the Conservatives

The view that conservatives are simply reactionary fails to take into account the political radicalism of some conservative politicians. While liberals and socialists are more likely to take a reformist position on key social issues — and embrace change for doctrinal rather than purely pragmatic reasons, conservatives are sometimes more willing than liberals and socialists to contemplate radical alternatives by breaking with existing political arrangements. This tendency becomes clear if we look at three examples of conservative political reforms.

Extension of the franchise

One of the most radical political changes of the nineteenth century in Britain was the Representation of the People Act (1867), introduced by the Conservative prime minister Benjamin Disraeli. Prior to 1867, the franchise was restricted to men of property, and the vast majority of the population could not vote. By excluding a majority of the population from elections, the parliamentary system remained in the hands of the upper middle classes and the aristocracy. Disraeli introduced the reform for two main reasons:

- He recognised the need to widen the parameters of political participation. Extending the right to vote would increase the legitimacy of the political system and integrate more voters into political society.
- By extending the franchise to middle-class voters, the Conservatives could broaden their political appeal. This strategy paid off, and the 1870s and 1880s were successful years for the Conservatives in electoral terms.

The extension of the franchise had a long-term impact on the British political system, ushering in a new era of mass party politics in which decision-making power began to shift away from parliament to the executive branch of government. By the time full universal adult suffrage was introduced in 1918 (1928 for women), politics in the UK had been transformed from its amateurish origins in the gentlemen's clubs of Pall Mall into a competitive electoral struggle between professional parties.

Civil service reform

A second example of radical Conservative reform is the change to the structure of the civil service introduced by Margaret Thatcher in the 1980s. Long an opponent of 'big government' and bureaucratic inertia, Thatcher brought in the former managing director of Marks and Spencer, Sir Derek Rayner, to consider ways of reducing the scale and organisation of the Whitehall machine. This led to the development of the 'Next Steps' reforms, which saw thousands of jobs contracted out to the private sector, and whole departments rationalised in an attempt to reduce costs and inefficiency. Although there was resistance to the changes, they created a new organisational culture at the heart of government, exemplified by the privatisation of the department traditionally responsible for the recruitment of Whitehall mandarins.

Trade union legislation

A third example of radical conservatism in action is the reform of industrial relations legislation during the Thatcher years, following a period of intense industrial unrest in the 1970s. Thatcher was particularly exercised by the economic cost of sustaining loss-making state enterprises, which were sold off to the private sector, leading to mass redundancies. In order to cope with the problem, and to increase the power of employers to deal with strikes, the Conservatives introduced a succession of laws banning secondary picketing (where a trade union not involved in a dispute calls a strike in a show of solidarity), and forcing union leaders to hold a secret ballot of members before going on strike. These changes radically altered the balance of power between capitalists and workers, introducing reforms that are still in operation today.

Conservatives and liberalism

In practical terms, therefore, conservatism cannot be described simply as a 'positional' (defensive) ideology, and conservatives do not exclusively place their faith in 'tried and tested' means. Although conservative politicians approach change from a non-doctrinal perspective, there are numerous cases of conservative parties embracing ideas from reformist political traditions such as liberalism.

This is particularly the case with the New Right, which moderated its defence of tradition in favour of increased individualism and economic freedom. Although this policy was unpopular among Tory paternalists in the UK (who

stressed the need for continuity and social stability), neoliberal New Right ideologues argued that the best guarantee of social stability lay in promoting increased efficiency and prosperity under the guidance of a strong state.

As we shall see in Chapter 5, the shift away from traditionalist values under the New Right has led to accusations that modern conservatives have in many respects abandoned their original principles in favour of right-wing liberalism. This reflects not only the increasing importance of the market as a basis of social order, but also the enduring importance of liberal values in western societies.

Conclusion

In conclusion, conservatives value authority and tradition for several reasons. Authority is seen as a vital resource for integrating societies — particularly during periods of rapid social and economic change when traditional institutions and structures are placed under stress. In the conservative philosophical tradition, authority is understood in terms of deference, shared identity and irrevocable obligation. Thinkers as different as Michael Oakeshott, Karl Popper and Arnold Gehlen stress the role of authority and tradition in the formation of stable human communities, emphasising the need to restrict the 'boundlessness' of human experience. This view has similarities with communitarianism, which seeks to challenge the individualist bias of Enlightenment rationalism. However, as we have seen, modern New Right conservatives are more sympathetic towards liberal individualism as a means for promoting economic growth and prosperity in market societies.

The conservative emphasis on tradition is variable. Many conservatives are simple traditionalists with a well-defined sentimental attachment to the past. Tradition is seen as a source of social integration and collective identity. As we saw in Chapter 1, however, conservatism is *not* just a question of sentiment or disposition: to equate conservatism with traditionalism is to equate a complex political ideology with nothing more than a stubborn attachment to outmoded ways of life and/or a fear of radical innovation.

The main preoccupation of conservatives is, rather, to preserve those structures and institutions that have stood the test of time. Conservatives advocate an evolutionary view of change as the 'normal accumulation of history', undistorted by radical experiments in social engineering. Although traditionalist conservatives clearly place great emphasis on the preservation of social and cultural traditions *for their own sake*, conservative politicians have repeatedly demonstrated themselves willing to tamper with tradition for pragmatic reasons. New Right politicians, in particular, introduced far-reaching changes in the 1980s in response to the changing needs of the market, in the process undermining many traditional ways of life.

Task 2.1

Conservatives believe that traditional institutions are controlled by 'bearers' of authority. Copy and complete the following table to explain the role and function of the institutions listed, and how they might contribute to the reproduction of authority relations.

Institution	Bearer of authority	Function in society
Family		
School		
Military		
Law		
Workplace		
Religion		

Guidance

Think about how institutions *confer* authority on those individuals who control them. Being in a position of authority gives people both *power* and *moral responsibility*. If people abuse their power, they forfeit their legitimacy, which in turn will reduce the likelihood of subordinates recognising their authority.

At the heart of all political theory is the problem of order and social cohesion. How does authority contribute to the stability and continuity of society? Conservatives favour institutions such as the family and religion because they have evolved largely without state guidance. On the other hand, institutions such as the law and the military embody social control and discipline, and their presence is designed to compensate for the breakdown of authority and social order.

Task 2.2

Read Source A and complete the questions that follow.

Source A

The desire to conserve is compatible with all manner of change, provided that change is also continuity. It has recently been argued with some force that the process of change in political life has become 'hyperactive'. Overstimulation of that shallow part of our being which constitutes the sum of our articulate
5   views has led to a profusion throughout the public realm of a sense that anything can and should be altered, together with proposals for reform, and political strategies, mounted by those within and by those without the institutions whose life they thereby threaten. This disease is of the kind which any conservative will attend to, first by trying to recognise its nature. The world
10   has become particularly 'opinionated', and in every corner of society people with neither the desire nor the ability to reflect on the social good are being asked to choose some favoured recipe for its realisation.

Roger Scruton, The Meaning of Conservatism (2001)

(a) What does the author mean when he insists that change should also be 'continuity' (line 2)?

(b) Why are conservatives sceptical of the rationalist view that anything can be altered (line 6)?

(c) To what extent is the conservative fear of 'opinionated' people evidence of scepticism about the value of democracy (line 10)?

Guidance

Remember *why* conservatives are reluctant to support random or unnecessary change, and what they hope to achieve by controlling the rate of change.

Opposition to rationalism stems from a suspicion that humans are unable to anticipate the full consequences of radical transformation or to control such consequences. For conservatives, it is much better to allow institutions (such as the family) to evolve through their own natural development.

Conservatives are hostile towards 'abstract intellectualism', preferring uncomplicated people with straightforward views and needs. They take the view that opinionated people have too many intellectual pretensions, which lead them to question received or conventional ways of life. Liberals and particularly Marxists place too much faith in 'grand theory' in an attempt to explain human social and economic life in terms of a single conceptual idea.

Useful websites

- For an in-depth analysis of conservatism and authority, see:
  www.newcriterion.com/archive/21/feb03/burke.htm
- On the conservative view of tradition, see:
  http://turnabout.ath.cx:8000/node/35
  www.nhinet.org/raeder.htm
- On disciplinarian conservatism, see:
  www.rockridgeinstitute.org/projects/strategic/nationasfamily/sfworldview

Further reading

- Adorno, T. W. et al. (1950) *The Authoritarian Personality*, Harper & Brothers.
- Freeden, M (1996) *Ideologies and Political Theory*, Oxford University Press.
- Raz, J. (ed.) (1990) *Authority*, New York University Press.
- Scruton, R. (1980) *The Meaning of Conservatism*, Penguin.

What is the place of the individual in conservative ideology?

Introduction

The place of the individual in conservative ideology is a common source of confusion. While early conservatism is characterised by a romantic idealisation of society as an 'organic whole', incorporating individuals within a dense network of ties and obligations, modern conservatism is more closely identified with a defence of individualism and economic freedom. To a large extent, this shift in perspective reflects the changing object of conservative critique in the nineteenth century and in the postwar era:

- Nineteenth-century paternalistic conservatives were exercised by hostility towards rapid modernisation and social change.
- Modern conservatives have been more concerned with the threat to individual (economic) freedom posed by the development of socialism.

There is a thus fault-line running through conservative political ideology, separating those committed to a pragmatic defence of conventional ways of life from those committed to a rationalist defence of the 'sovereign individual of capitalism'. Although there are many shades of opinion between the twin extremes of paternalistic traditionalism and bourgeois individualism, most conservatives fall into one or other camp.

In what follows, we will examine the different views of traditionalists and individualists on the place of the individual in conservative ideology, and the value of the community as a source of identity and purpose. Whereas traditional conservatives depict the nation as an 'organic' entity that is greater than the sum of its parts, bourgeois individualists adopt a more atomistic perspective, viewing society in a more modern way as an 'aggregation of individuals'.

Why do traditionalist conservatives believe in an 'organic' concept of society?

In social and political philosophy, the term holism means the opposite of atomism. It conveys the idea that societies must be examined as a whole rather than from the perspective of individual agents. This is because individuals are ontologically inseparable from the community that gives them life. In other words, their existence and frame of reference is unintelligible in isolation from the community of which they are a constituent element, and without which they would not be able to live a meaningful existence.

The development of the organic metaphor

The theory of society as an 'organic whole' has a long and distinguished heritage in English and European conservative thought. The idea is perhaps most developed in the German conservative tradition, which in the nineteenth century was more reactionary and romantic than English Toryism. In order to understand the appeal of 'organicism' in political theory, it is necessary to understand, first, the holistic logic of the biological analogy, and, second, the hostility of conservatives towards abstract intellectualism.

Proponents of the organic analogy stress the similarity between the national community and a biological organism. This view can be summarised as follows: societies — like natural organisms — should be considered as unified wholes. Just as the biological organism is dependent on the correct functioning of all of its constituent parts, so societies must be thought of as interdependent wholes. If one part of the organism/community is damaged, the correct functioning of the whole will be affected.

The organic metaphor contains another proviso: namely, that human societies develop and evolve naturally, not through rational design. As was evident in Oakeshott's critique of rationalism in politics, conservatives like to defend the natural order of society by refuting the possibility of radical change. Societies should, instead, be compared to 'ancient trees', any alteration of which will destroy their natural development.

The organic metaphor has its roots in romanticism, a school of thought that developed in central Europe from the late eighteenth century onwards. There are three elements to this:

- Conservative organic society theorists such as Johann Gottfried von Herder (1744–1803) criticised the liberal conception of political association derived from John Locke, according to which society is essentially a contractual entity comprised of individuals pursuing their own private goals, who only cooperate in the expectation of mutual advantage. Like Jean-Jacques Rousseau, Herder argued that the atomistic theory of society devalues politics by placing artificial limits on civic association, thereby reducing the sovereign power of the community to determine its identity and collective purpose.

- According to organic society theorists, the atomistic perspective ignores the qualitative distinction between forms of civic association such as clubs, federations and cultural organisations, and higher-level political forms of association such as nations, which impose binding obligations on their members. In the liberal theory of society, this qualitative distinction is lost, undermining the possibility of national integration.

- According to organic society theorists, traditional contract theory is flawed because it overlooks the fact that membership of a nation is an involuntary form of allegiance. Except for immigrants who choose to move to another state, membership of a particular community is less a 'voluntary act' based on choice or free will than a process of integration into an indivisible whole. Organic society theorists advocate an approach to political organisation based on a cultural definition of communal participation. Ideally, full integration requires individuals to abandon any claims to 'natural rights' (i.e. rights they may claim outside or beyond those which flow from a specific community) in order to promote full identification and participation. The organic metaphor implies that through participation — for example, through cultural participation or shared language codes, individuals become 'embedded' in their community, which acquires a significance and status beyond the abstract ties that govern association between autonomous individuals in liberal societies.

This idea finds expression in the work of **Hegel** (1770–1831), who recognised the weakness of the liberal theory of the state. Hegel criticised the atomistic, cosmopolitan tendency in liberalism, which presents an 'ideal humanity' fundamentally at odds with the cultural and historical traditions of actual nations. He advocated the idea of a 'national spirit' as a means for binding individuals within communities based on shared identity and purpose.

In the organic society, therefore, the community is celebrated as a superior, overarching entity that transcends the natural rights of the individual. The preference is for an assertion of common identity and unified purpose, without which collectivities such as nations lack the cohesion and sense of moral purpose necessary to prosper as a unified entity. This idea is, of course, criticised by liberal and libertarian philosophers, who continue to defend a theory of association based on natural rights and voluntary association. Critics of romanticism argue the following:

- The metaphysical basis of the holistic view of society is dubious and its consequences are unpredictable. The fixation with a 'national image', based on clearly identifiable ethnic, cultural and linguistic features, exaggerates the real or potential homogeneity of human communities and is clearly hostile to the kind of tolerant cosmopolitanism advocated by Immanuel Kant.
- The fixation with identity led to an anti-modernist 'revolt against reason' in German culture and philosophy, which laid the foundations for the rise of neocorporatist and fascist ideologies in the twentieth century. Corporatism in its original form was a theory of political organisation based on the idea that society is made up of 'corporations' which mediate between the state and the individual, and promote social harmony and integration. In fascist ideologies, neocorporatism was an updated, 'national-populist' form of collectivism which sought to reconcile capitalism with national-economic goals. In fascism, the organicist ideal of a traditional community (*Gemeinschaft*) based on affective bonds was set against the complex, cosmopolitan reality of modern society (*Gesellschaft*), with disastrous political consequences.

In middle-way English conservatism, the metaphor of the organic society is less evident. Although paternalistic Tories reject the idea of unfettered individualism, the liberal character of English conservative thought is much stronger, and English national identity is defined more by a cultural attachment to *class* than by an *ethnic* attachment to the 'folk community'. This is one reason why the Conservative Party has been largely free of right-wing extremism throughout its history. Most English conservatives see fascism as a failed totalitarian experiment, based on the same unworkable collectivist ideals as communism: when politicians begin to speak in terms of the 'higher rationality' of the state over society, the chief victim is usually personal liberty.

Hence the more pragmatic approach to the place of the individual in modern conservative ideologies. Modern conservatives reassert the bonds of nation and community, but also emphasise freedom in a negative sense as freedom from coercion. This atomistic approach has developed into a core

theme of New Right ideology, which privileges the sovereign individual of capitalism above pseudo-collectivist concepts of society as an 'organic whole'.

Hostility to intellectual abstraction

Another feature of traditional conservatism is hostility to intellectualism. Traditional conservatives have a preference for traditional forms of social knowledge, and see abstract rationalist thought as depersonalised and decommunalised: that is, removed from its social and historical context. According to Mannheim (1986), this implies an indifference towards 'all the sensitivities to knowledge which render the world comprehensible to the subject but which do not at the same time make that comprehension universally communicable'.

What this means is that the practical, social knowledge of the community is undermined by the abstract character of scientific rationality. The 'felt' historical and social reality of the community is diminished by the indifferent march of reason, which imposes a rational agenda on previously self-generating and self-regulating ways of thinking and being. Gradually, the integrity of the organic community is undermined, which in turn threatens centuries-old customs and traditions. These can never be reclaimed, so must be defended as integral components of the organic society.

For liberals, the problem with this view is that it can result in the use of arbitrary coercion to defend a particular set of social arrangements merely because they exist and are deemed worthy of defending by those in positions of authority. But if such a defence is based on conviction rather than reason, it risks being accepted even though it may be anachronistic or nonsensical. In these circumstances, the preference for a substantive defence of what is 'good' for the community is purchased at the price of being false, undermining social progress and human emancipation.

This point is summarised by Hayek in a famous essay on conservatism. Although sympathetic to certain aspects of conservatism, which he saw as less objectionable than socialism, Hayek (1960) observed that the worst feature of the conservative attitude is its 'propensity to reject well-substantiated new knowledge because it dislikes some of the consequences which seem to follow from it'.

In the modern world, however, it is largely impossible to ignore the influence of scientific reason, and certainly impossible to ignore the impact of individualism and secularisation. No society can remain a 'closed system' for long, excluding those truths it does not like. In the long run, such a strategy can only result in social stagnation and cultural decline.

Why, and to what extent, do conservatives believe in one-nation principles?

The idea that the community is like a biological organism that must be protected from harmful internal and external influences is an important feature of paternalistic/corporatist theories of society, but does not retain this central significance in modern conservatism. It is important to be clear about the reasons for this transition, which is closely tied to the changing view of the individual in conservative ideology.

One-nation conservatism and social integration

An important point for one-nation conservatives is that state intervention — and thus, by definition, state coercion — is seen as a legitimate means of protecting established political arrangements and reconciling conflicting interests. Both paternalistic conservatism and socialism are more likely than liberalism to make claims on the individual, and infringe the protected sphere of individual freedom.

However, although there are similarities in their holistic approach, the organic theory of society at the heart of one-nation conservatism must not be confused with the socialist commitment to rational reform and state planning as the means for transforming society through social engineering. Paternalistic conservatism is based on a neocorporatist theory of the state, which emphasises the need for traditional leadership (social rank, hierarchy, authority), social cohesion, state intervention to stabilise the market (managed capitalism) and the promotion of civic association.

Paternalism entails a system of rule based on benevolent elitism, whereby established elites (the 'recognisably superior elements' in society) rule on behalf of the people by virtue of their relative wisdom, experience and social status. The paternalistic ethos is in part determined by the nature of representative democracy, which, as an indirect form of democratic rule, successfully reconciles elite rule with limited popular participation. The system came to fruition in the UK in the nineteenth century, and epitomises the pragmatic tendency in traditional English Toryism under Benjamin Disraeli.

Paternalistic conservatives stress the idea of natural inequality, according to which those with superior wisdom, experience and social status have a right and duty to rule on behalf of the common people, who cannot be responsible for their

low station in life. Intrinsic to this elitist ideology is, therefore, the notion of social rank — an idea associated with Edmund Burke. He rejected the possibility of social equality, believing that individuals must accept their status and rank within the social order, and that social order itself is dependent on individuals 'knowing their place' and not upsetting the 'natural order of things'.

Under Disraeli, paternalism was officially characterised as 'one-nation' conservatism, based on the argument that membership of a single nation (the 'English') was more significant than membership of a particular social class. Disraeli considered that the Conservatives should seek to represent all Englishmen and women rather than just the socially privileged. This reflected a pragmatic view that it was more sensible to integrate the lower social classes into political society by offering limited reforms and material aid.

Modern conservatives in the twentieth century have continued many Disraelian themes, although they have gradually abandoned his commitment to social integration. Under Winston Churchill and Harold Macmillan, the Conservatives gave their qualified acceptance to the postwar social-democratic consensus as a means of reconciling the opposing interests of employers and trade unions. In the decades following 1945, the UK entered an unprecedented period of prosperity with all indicators showing an improvement in living conditions and welfare. Indeed, many conservatives look back on the period as a 'golden age' in which the class conflict and economic instability of the interwar years was replaced by a more equitable system of wealth distribution and collective endeavour.

One-nation conservatism and the defence of inequality

Despite the progressive nature of postwar development, it would be wrong to mistake the one-nation commitment to social integration for a commitment to social equality.

Egalitarianism is a collectivist ideal, which goes beyond the traditional liberal view that all individuals have equal worth and that all individuals should be treated equally. Egalitarianism translates into a commitment to positive equality: namely, a belief that the purpose of politics is to promote 'equality of outcomes' in order to compensate for the undeserved natural and social inequalities of human beings.

According to the egalitarian view, no individual 'deserves' to suffer because he or she was born with inadequate resources or talents — even if the individual in question is the type of person who would not naturally be inclined to develop his or her energies to the full. The capacity of individuals to make full use of available talents may be impaired by other forms of social inequality, which reduce their ability to compete in a highly competitive marketplace. If, for example, a working-class couple has limited economic and cultural capital, their children will not be able to compete as effectively as children from middle-class households.

For those who advocate equality of opportunity and equality of outcomes, the purpose of politics should be to design a system of distribution to ensure that no individual is denied equal access to what John Rawls terms 'primary goods', such as liberty and opportunity, income and the bases of self-respect. Rawls (1971) wrote that all primary goods should be 'distributed equally unless an unequal distribution of any or all of these goods is to the advantage of the least favoured'. In other words, unless there are universally valid reasons for preserving some forms of inequality (because they actually benefit society as a whole), all individuals should have an equal right of access to those basic resources that enable everyone to compete on an equal basis.

The conservative approach to equality is very different from this. In opposition to the liberal view of equality, that all humans should be treated equally, and the socialist view of equality, that we should strive to achieve an equality of outcomes, at the root of the conservative attitude is a basic preference for property freedom: namely, the equal freedom of all individuals of all social classes to possess private property and to dispose of their resources as they wish. This idea lies at the heart of conservative ideology — not just because private property is viewed as a cornerstone of social order, but because property ownership is a basic condition for the preservation of existing forms of rank, privilege and inherited social power.

In his analysis of conservative thought, Ted Honderich identifies the following conservative objections to the principle of equality of outcomes:

- Inequality is rarely as bad as reformers argue: all poverty is relative, and even the poor in western societies are comparatively well-off.
- The demand for inequality is based on envy and resentment: not everyone can have the finer things in life, and egalitarians should accept this fact.
- The idea of a society in which everyone is equal is unnatural: societies have evolved organically into their current form and any radical alteration would be harmful.
- The idea of egalitarianism is preposterous and will never be achieved, given the way humans covet wealth and status.
- Egalitarianism results in 'terrible uniformity', which threatens traditional identities and social differences by promising to homogenise society (Honderich 2005).

Although these arguments are hardly conclusive (and rehearse a well-worn perspective on human nature), they ground some of the core assumptions of

New Right conservatism, particularly the libertarian conservative view that egalitarianism is inconsistent with human nature because it undermines the motivation necessary to encourage ambition and achievement. If human beings were all equal — if there were no legitimate social or economic differences between individuals — this would destroy the structure of incentives and rewards upon which capitalism is based.

How do New Right theorists view the individual?

At the centre of libertarian New Right ideology is a commitment to the free market, predicated on the natural inequality of individuals. For New Right thinkers, the one-nation ideal is inconsistent not only with economic freedom (see Chapter 4), but also with human nature. The starting point for New Right ideology is not the cultural or institutional fabric of society, but the marketplace. Whereas one-nation conservatives see society as a hierarchy of privileges and obligations, in New Right conservative ideology the cultural and institutional fabric of society is simply the context within which individual agents collide and combine for their own individual advantage.

Methodological individualism

This atomistic view is based on a philosophical outlook known as methodological individualism, which has its source in classical economic theory. Pioneers of methodological individualism, such as the economist Adam Smith (1723–90) and the sociologist Max Weber, argue that collectivities such as 'society' can only be understood as the sum of actual or possible actions of individuals. In other words, 'societies' — as aggregations of individuals — are not conceptually distinct from the individuals who comprise them. The idea that the 'whole is greater than the sum of its parts' — and that individuals have some collective identity beyond simple ties to family and nation — is rejected as nonsensical.

In this respect, the New Right outlook substitutes a 'thin' concept of the exchange society for the 'thick' concept of organic society in traditional paternalistic conservatism, reducing to an absolute minimum the properties of society as an entity. Whereas traditional conservatives identify the organic community as a historical continuity that imposes identity and belonging on individual subjects, the libertarian conservative view imports an abstract conception of the public purpose as a function of the sum of individual private motivations and actions.

From this perspective there is no 'plural subject', only individual agents, the sum of whose transactions constitute the material reality of society. Society exists only as a cognitive idea in the minds of thinking individuals, whose ties and obligations are determined by choice rather than being imposed on them by the community of which they are members.

This 'thin' concept of society is necessarily somewhat bleak, as it reduces society to a population of individuals who only take account of one another in order to avoid unnecessary or unpleasant collisions. It strips away all those vague concepts of community and cooperation that do not fit into the matrix of contractual ties and obligations into which individuals voluntarily enter. Although there must be mutual awareness of the way freely transacting individuals view one another (there must, after all, be language and culture, which exist before the actual or possible actions of individuals), social interaction becomes a question of private choice rather than duty or obligation. In political terms, this effectively reduces the public sphere to the administration of those essential services (such as justice and defence) which freely transacting individuals cannot organise independently or privately.

Rational choice theory

This perspective has been elaborated in neoclassical economics using the framework of rational choice theory. Theorists who employ this method argue that social order and cooperation can only be understood as the outcome of interactions between individuals in pursuit of private self-interest. All individuals are depicted as rational agents with limited resource endowments, each capable of making sovereign decisions on the basis of available information. Although *self-interested*, individuals are not necessarily *selfish* (for example, some might give to charity). However, the motivation for action is always the same: namely, the pursuit of self-interest either by cooperating or by competing under specific social and economic conditions. Consequently, giving to charity can be explained not as a form of altruism but as an autonomous action that either:

● increases the moral self-esteem of the donor, or
● increases the probability that others will also give

In effect, the rational actor will only cooperate if he or she is convinced of the advantage to be gained, and if he or she is convinced that others in a similar position will act in a reciprocal fashion.

Thus, while reciprocity requires trust in order to reduce free riding, where individuals defect from a cooperative scheme or fail to honour their obligations, such trust can be sustained through the long-term generation of ties of interdependence. This argument can be traced back ultimately to Adam Smith. However, it is also linked to Emile Durkheim (1858–1917), who observed that the division of labour in modern societies is a necessary means of promoting interdependence in the absence of traditional forms of mechanical solidarity (where people have natural ties linking them together).

Evaluation

It is clear that there is a tension between traditional and New Right conservatism concerning the position of the individual in society. Traditional conservatives accept a much greater degree of responsibility for the welfare of the community, whereas New Right conservatives emphasise the need for self-reliance.

However, a consistent theme running through conservative ideology is an implicit defence of natural and social inequality. As we have seen, traditional conservatives express a preference for the natural inequality of humans, seeing no contradiction between inherited natural and social advantage and the social iniquity of the wealth divide that characterises most societies. In the modern era, however, it has become less acceptable to advocate inequality in explicit terms. For New Right conservatives, it is necessary to justify the persistence of inequality by other means.

Most people understand and accept that social inequality exists, and many would concede that such inequalities have their roots in socioeconomic factors such as class, wealth and social status. But few people would be prepared to accept an explicit justification for inequality without some way of linking unequal shares to a positive idea of freedom or progress.

Robert Eccleshall (2001) argues that, whereas equality is central to the language and ideology of socialism, New Right conservatives tend to use a form of **double coding** as a means of 'decontesting the shared concepts of political discourse by attaching them with ideologically specific meaning'. New Right conservatives, in his view, are obliged to camouflage their commitment to inequality by shuffling 'their furniture around to conceal the principal items within'.

This double coding serves not only to obscure the implicit defence of inequality in New Right ideology, but also to resolve the essential tension between its more traditional neoconservative and neoliberal wings. The appropriation of libertarian ideas in the 1970s and 1980s was not welcomed by all conservatives. Some were angered by the tendency of neoliberals to depict society as an empty shell within which private individuals engage in competitive exchange.

Although the metaphor of organic society was clearly outdated for the New Right, neoconservative elements found it difficult to accept the full implications of the Thatcherite view that there is 'no such thing as society, only individuals and their families' without an explicit commitment to the second (and less frequently cited) clause of her statement.

The subtext of this statement is the idea that 'charity begins at home'. This nineteenth-century proverb holds that giving to the needy and the poor is fundamentally a question of choice, and should thus not be organised by the state. An individual may wish to give for pragmatic or philanthropic reasons, but this choice should be up to the person concerned rather than state administrators. The individual's first duty should be to their own family, placing a particular responsibility on the male breadwinner as material provider, father-figure and head of the household — women are assigned a less public role as household managers.

Margaret Thatcher — no ordinary housewife

A solution was thus found to the tension within New Right ideology. The rhetoric of 'Victorian values' was designed to bridge the divide between paternalism and libertarianism by redefining freedom in terms of economic opportunity and property ownership. Whereas Tory paternalists had been prepared to accept a broader role for the state in the organisation of society, the libertarian ethos of bourgeois individualism appealed to the Victorian ideal of self-reliance as a means of reducing the cost of state intervention and public ownership.

The appeal of this idea of Victorian values lies in the way freedom is delimited as a function of economic activity. Private individuals, it is stressed, are freer and more responsible when they are allowed (or required) to assume control over their own economic livelihood. The Victorian era was one of immense economic achievement, based on both the entrepreneurial ethos of late-nineteenth-century business and the abundant material resources of the British empire.

By reasserting the relevance of the philanthropic, dutiful capitalist in the modern age, the New Right found a convenient method for legitimising the needs of the present in terms of the past.

Conclusion

Having examined a range of conservative theories of society, it is possible to conclude our discussion by asking: *to what extent is there a tension between the conservative commitment to individual economic freedom and commitment to the community?*

It should now be clear that an essential dualism lies at the heart of conservative ideology, centred on the status and role of the individual in society. This dualism is responsible for producing a tension in modern conservatism, which conservative politicians in Europe and North America have yet to resolve, despite recent efforts to locate a middle-way between organicism and individualism. As modern conservatism has absorbed the economic and political doctrines of fiscal prudence, economic laissez faire and competitive individualism, so it has altered the basic foundations of its own belief in an organic moral and social order. In this respect, there has been a radical departure from the early corporatist origins of conservative ideology, and few modern-day conservatives now subscribe to such outmoded views.

However, a tension clearly remains and, as we shall see in the next two chapters, there are good reasons to believe that some elements of modern conservative ideology are based on irreconcilable premises. This has not prevented conservative parties from trying to adapt their ideological approach to accommodate such contradictions. In the UK, for example, the Conservatives have tried to emulate the rhetoric of compassionate conservatism popular among neoconservatives in the USA. Compassionate conservatives believe that:

- Government should have a limited role in people's lives: unrestricted competition is the best means of achieving social progress.
- Government should promote prosperity rather than entitlement: although the prosperity created by the market leaves many impoverished, the government has no responsibility to redistribute wealth to those who are not fully incentivised to accumulate wealth for themselves.
- Government should act only as a provider of last resort.

The ideology of compassionate conservatism is based on an optimistic belief in people's ability to overcome adversity, which contrasts starkly with the traditionalist belief that society has a duty to protect the weak. Believers in compassionate conservatism argue that social welfare *disempowers* those in need by giving them less control over their own lives, and that preventing the more affluent from acquiring more wealth only serves to increase rather than reduce poverty. However, there is little evidence to suggest that unconstrained market capitalism benefits the poorer in society. On the contrary, economic data demonstrate an increasing disparity rather than an approximation of wealth in the USA and UK in the last two decades.

Economic statistics, however, are not the primary issue. The important point is the *coherence* of the ideological strategy that modern conservatives employ to overcome the tension between personal wealth creation and the general welfare of the community.

As Ted Honderich argues (2005), the idea that unconstrained wealth creation is a necessary condition for raising the material welfare of society as a whole is relevant only to counter *egalitarian* objections. Wherever New Right conservatives are unconcerned with combating egalitarian claims, he argues, 'their end result is spoken of mainly in terms of individuals having the rewards of their labour or of the risks they take with their money'.

What does this mean? It means that the *principal* target of conservative ideology has traditionally been the egalitarian ideals of socialism. However, given that egalitarianism, has to all intents and purposes, been defeated as an alternative to centre-right ideology, conservatives have switched their emphasis towards a Lockean defence of the *right of individuals to appropriate the full value of their personal labour*.

We can see the tension between defence of individual economic freedom and defence of social stability by looking at recent developments in the UK Conservative Party:

- Under Michael Howard, the Conservatives advanced an aggressively anti-tax agenda that failed to inspire voters, who were sceptical about the possibility of funding social welfare with a severely diminished level of tax revenues.

- His successor, David Cameron, has adopted a more cautious approach based on the assumption that voters (in the UK at least) will punish parties that fail to guarantee state health and welfare provision. David Cameron's brand of middle-way conservatism is clearly designed to appeal beyond the core Conservative voters in the UK (particularly to female voters).

David Cameron

But can modern conservatives bridge the divide between their commitment to individual self-enrichment and social responsibility?

It remains an issue for many conservatives that the 'trickle-down' effect does not in fact improve the general welfare of the community. Yet, unless conservatives are prepared to move back towards some form of interventionism based on a tripartite system of economic management (where the state acts as 'ringmaster', balancing the competing interests of capital and labour), it is

difficult to see how the Conservatives can realise any promise to control the power of business and finance.

Many conservatives in the UK continue to argue that the state should act to prevent the kind of socioeconomic polarisation that bedevils US society. Although this does not commit UK conservatives to egalitarianism, it does rehearse the once uncontroversial view that the ruling class has a moral duty to guide and help those who are poor through no fault of their own. Yet this is a view that is incompatible with the neoliberal belief in property freedom, according to which no individual should be prevented from aspiring to or acquiring unlimited material wealth.

In Chapter 4, we will attempt to understand the reasons for the shift towards a neoliberal defence of economic freedom and private property in conservative ideology. There were economic and political reasons for the revival of conservative fortunes in the 1980s, and these must be understood before we can fully grasp the contradictions between the neoliberal and neoconservative dimensions of modern conservatism.

Task 3.1

Read Source A and complete the questions that follow.

Source A

Hegel finds the unity of individual satisfaction and freedom in conformity to the social ethos of the organic community. [...An] organic community fosters those desires that most benefit the community. Moreover it so imbues its members with the sense that their own identity consists in being part of a
5   community that they will no more think of going off in pursuit of their own private interests than one part of the organism that is my body — say, my left arm — would think of hiving off my shoulder to find something better to do than stuff my mouth with food. Nor should we forget that the relationship between an organism and its parts is reciprocal. I need my left arm and my
10   left arm needs me. The organic community will no more disregard the interests of its members than I would disregard an injury to my left arm.

Peter Singer, *Hegel* (1983)

(a) Why do 'organic society' theorists draw an analogy between human societies and the biological organisms?

(b) Why do conservative thinkers such as Hegel believe that an 'organic community fosters those desires that most benefit the community' (lines 2–3)?

(c) Organic society theorists argue that an organic community fosters group solidarity, so that individuals would *not want* to act in ways inconsistent with the needs and interests of the community. How realistic is this view?

Task 3.1 (continued)

Guidance

Recall that organic society theorists such as Hegel believe that communities, just like biological organisms, should be considered as *unified wholes*: just as biological organisms are dependent on the correct working of all their constituent parts, so societies should be seen as interdependent wholes. If one part of the organism/community is damaged, this will affect the correct functioning of the whole, undermining its overall cohesion.

Liberals point to the conformist and authoritarian consequences of organicist theories. They argue that such forms of conservatism end up imposing an identity on members of the community, giving rulers the power to override independent initiative and alternative ways of life. They suggest that it is ultimately unrealistic to believe that, in modern societies, individuals would only want to act in ways that serve the interests of the community as a whole.

Task 3.2

Explain the New Right objections to egalitarianism by copying and completing the following table.

Objection	Explanation
Inequality is relative	
Egalitarianism is based on resentment	
Egalitarianism undermines ambition	
Egalitarianism requires continual redistribution if it is to work	
Egalitarianism results in 'uniformity'	

Task 3.2 (continued)

Guidance

Remember that opposition to equality may be framed in terms that emphasise the social importance of inequality. Some libertarian conservatives believe that any attempt to enforce equal treatment and/or equal outcomes is a threat to individual choice and freedom. States can use their coercive power to promote equality, but this is essentially an 'unnatural' state of affairs.

Conservatives are primarily interested in defending the *existing* distribution of social resources. 'Just' distributions take little account of the different talents, aspirations and dispositions that individuals have, and no redistribution of wealth can ever be 'final'.

Useful websites

- On the conservative attitude towards change, see:
  www.bigissueground.com/politics/ash-conservatismchange.shtml

Further reading

- Eccleshall, R. (2001) 'The doing of conservatism', in M. Freeden, Reassessing *Political Ideologies: The Durability of Dissent*, Taylor & Francis.
- Hayek, F. (1960) 'Why I am not a conservative', in *The Constitution of Liberty*, Routledge & Kegan Paul.
- Honderich, T. (2005) *Conservatism: Burke, Nozick, Bush, Blair?*, Pluto Press.
- Mannheim, K. (1986) *Conservatism: A Contribution to the Sociology of Knowledge*, Routledge.
- Rawls, J. (1971) *A Theory of Justice*, Harvard University Press.

What are the ideological origins of the New Right?

Introduction

As will be clear from the previous chapter, one of the central problems in modern conservatism concerns the legitimacy of state intervention in the economy. It has been shown that a tension exists between paternalism and libertarianism in New Right ideology, and that this tension has resulted in a contradictory emphasis on both economic freedom and social stability.

In this chapter we will look at the political and economic reasons for the rise of the New Right, and examine in greater detail the economic and philosophical arguments put forward by theorists of the New Right to justify a withdrawal of the state from management of the economy and the abolition of public ownership. At the centre of this political strategy is a commitment to property freedom, based on a belief in private enterprise, reduced state intervention and deregulated labour markets. Drawing on the classical liberal arguments of John Locke and Adam Smith, New Right theorists argue for a radical alteration in the balance of power between the individual and the state in the determination of economic outcomes.

The logic of their arguments must, however, be placed in the context of economic developments in the 1970s, when the period of postwar growth and prosperity came to an end. This period was characterised by increasing political polarisation in the capitalist societies of the West, as the left began to demand a further transfer of economic decision making away from private business into the hands of the state. This radicalisation of politics alarmed conservatives on both sides of the Atlantic, fuelling demands for a more concerted defence of the principles of market capitalism.

In what follows, therefore, we will begin by examining the changing nature of conservative justifications for private property and economic freedom.

Although there is a basic continuity in the way traditional and New Right conservatives defend property and privilege, New Right theorists have formulated a more rigorous and explicitly ideological justification for inequality derived from libertarian political philosophy. Once we have grasped the philosophical basis of New Right ideology, we will be in a better position to understand, first, the revival of conservative fortunes in the 1980s, and second, the political–economic logic of New Right conservatism.

How and why have conservatives sought to justify private property?

There are basic strategies open to conservatives to justify private property. The first is based on the idea that property is *sacred*, something that bestows certain qualities on owners through the fact of their possession or inheritance. This idea is commonly associated with traditional conservatives, who see property as essentially a *material extension of the self*. The second strategy is indebted to the liberal rationalism of philosophers such as John Locke, according to whom ownership of property is an inalienable right, and a basic condition of liberty.

Traditionalist justifications for property

In traditional conservatism, property is viewed as a logical extension of the self. From a conservative perspective, property provides social status and economic power; it also increases the personal security of the individual, giving him or her a level of protection against the intrusive power of the state. Although the conditions of its original acquisition (that is, the circumstances under which one person acquires land or property at the expense of another person) are largely irrelevant for conservatives, the idea of legitimate claim rights is fundamental.

For example, a feudal lord in the fourteenth century held sway over his land and its inhabitants, either because the land was granted to him in exchange for services rendered to the king or because he acquired it through conquest, at the expense of another landowner. Whether either of these justifications for ownership can be seen as legal or legitimate is a historical question that ceases to matter once a *de facto* claim-right to ownership has been established over time. The feudal lord simply owns the land in question because he always has done and the local people acknowledge or acquiesce in his claim.

For the traditional conservative, then, entitlement bestows certain powers and duties on the property owner. The feudal lord (a social role now largely extinct in Europe) could charge farmers' rent to use his land; but he also incurred certain seigneurial obligations that derived from his status as lord and master — for example, arbitrating in local conflicts. Such obligations are integral to the structure of authority in society, providing a stable basis for social order, rank and privilege.

For traditional conservatives, therefore, property has a sacred quality, but also implies some form of social duty or obligations. As we saw in the previous chapter, this idea is connected to paternalistic concepts of noblesse oblige, whereby privilege brings with it responsibilities.

In capitalist societies, however, the main form of private property is not land but capital. Wealth is accumulated by entrepreneurs and investors for private gain, granting them a level of social power unavailable to those without equivalent means. In the Victorian era, the great surplus wealth of industrialists was often invested by philanthropic capitalists in social projects for the betterment of the working class. Schemes such as the Peabody Trust built cheap tenements for workers employed in local industries, which bestowed 'benefactor' status on the philanthropists concerned. This in turn increased their esteem and moral authority within society, as well as imposing discipline on workers, part of whose wages were returned to the capitalist in return for cheap subsidised accommodation.

New Right theories of property freedom

The rise of the New Right is closely connected with an intellectual shift away from social liberalism among political philosophers and social scientists in Europe and the USA in the 1970s. This shift was at first confined to a handful of economists grouped around the Chicago School, including Milton Friedman and Mancur Olson. These thinkers were concerned with the limits of Keynesian-welfarist solutions to economic management — particularly the problem of inflation. However, their assault on the postwar social-democratic consensus revealed a deeper hostility towards egalitarian and collectivist principles, which gradually found its way into the intellectual mainstream in Europe and the USA.

This hostility was fuelled by the emerging crisis of hegemony in the liberal-capitalist system of the West, as more people began to question the basic principles of the 'marketplace' model of society. In the atmosphere of anti-communism that pervaded during the Cold War period, many conservatives and liberals were concerned that criticism of the marketplace society could undermine individual economic freedom and the power and influence of corporate capitalism.

The libertarianism of Robert Nozick

One of the most famous exponents of right-wing libertarianism is the US philosopher Robert Nozick (1940–95), whose classic study *Anarchy, State and Utopia* (1974) contains a powerful justification for the preservation of inequality based on the defence of liberty. Nozick argues that the redistribution of wealth not only reduces the liberty of individuals but is also pointless and harmful to society.

First, egalitarianism undermines the principle that individuals can and should be able to invest, spend or otherwise dispose of their assets as and how they wish, without their being subject to external infringement or taxation by the state. If individuals want to spend their money on making sports stars or celebrities richer, then it is within their rights to do so. For the state to prevent them, or to appropriate some portion of celebrities' assets on the grounds that wealth must be distributed equally to the community as a whole, is an infringement of the liberty of those parties who voluntarily entered into a given transaction for their own personal or mutual advantage.

Second, wealth redistribution is also pointless, because without continual redistribution some individuals are inevitably going to acquire more than others, either through hard work or by some other means. The existing pattern of distribution in capitalist societies reflects a long history of acquisition, exchange and transaction between private individuals based on legitimate claim rights. For the state to intervene in order to alter these arrangements is futile because all future acquisition, exchange and transaction would have to be continually monitored and adjusted in order to maintain an equitable distribution of assets in line with egalitarian principles. The state would, in effect, be forced to redistribute wealth continually in order to perpetuate an unattainable and unnatural status quo.

Third, redistribution is harmful because it ignores the functional importance of inequality for the maintenance of social order based on competitive exchange. In a society based on equality of outcomes, people would have nothing to strive for and ambition and innovation would be stifled.

In place of coercive taxation, Nozick recommends a radical proprietist solution to the problems of economic and political organisation. In this utopian scheme, individuals would buy into those cooperative schemes ('protective associations') of their own free choosing. A minimal state would be preserved for the purpose of civil defence and adjudicating in contractual disputes, and it would have no economic role.

Like Friedrich Hayek and Murray Rothbard (1926–95), Nozick stresses the utility of competitive exchange as the cornerstone of social order, effectively negating the notion of 'social justice'. According to this view, there is nothing just or unjust about inequalities produced by the market. The rules of distribution are a 'lottery' that cannot be controlled by interventionist governments. The practical implications of this anarchocapitalist approach are clear: the view that governments should intervene in order to determine economic outcomes is a mistaken one, for the distribution of resources by means of rational planning and/or compensatory welfare is inconsistent with the *de facto* evolution of private property relations. Individuals may have moral qualms about the social inequalities in market societies, but their moral concern is misplaced because competitive exchange has no ethical dimension.

In fact, for Nozick and others, the attempt by states to redistribute the assets of private individuals is itself immoral because it constitutes a form of forced labour: requiring people to part with a percentage of their wealth effectively amounts to requiring them to hand over a portion of their labour for nothing. Even though some rich individuals may earn a hundred times the wage of poor individuals with no assets, libertarians view redistribution as socially legitimised theft.

Classical liberalism

Notwithstanding the practical limitations of Nozick's anarchocapitalist views, his defence of private property exemplifies the basic logic of the New Right conservative perspective on property. This perspective is derived from classical liberalism, and revolves around the view that:

- ownership of private property symbolises individual rights in a concrete form
- all individuals have an equal right to own property and dispose of it as they wish

The intellectual origins of this idea are often associated with the philosophy of John Locke, who argued that individuals should be allowed to enjoy the fruits of their labour. Locke's argument can be summarised by a simple example. In a metaphysical sense, the person who digs a well invests the material object of their labour (the well) with something of themselves. The economic worth of this labour can then be recovered in the form of value or profit; for example, if the digger of the well decides to sell water to neighbouring farmers.

The inalienable quality of property — the idea that it cannot be taken away — serves as an incentive for individuals to invest. If individuals believe they cannot enjoy the fruits of their labour (or receive a return on their investments), they will be discouraged from making such commitments. Similarly, without security of tenure a farmer will not be inclined to work the soil. For this reason, property rights and property law are vitally important in capitalist societies, providing a legal regulatory framework for the contractual arrangements and complex transactions that constitute the economic fabric of commerce and industry.

Social status versus egalitarianism

Within neoliberal ideology there is an implicit assumption that property rights are, or should be, *unrelated to socioeconomic class*. If individuals possess assets, this gives them the ability to enjoy privileges regardless of the status of their family. Although an individual's background may be relevant to their cultural identity (and therefore to their sense of belonging within a community), the nature of their class or ethnicity is irrelevant to their status as economic agents concerned with private advantage. In a formal sense, therefore, there should be no legal or other constraint on the right of individuals to exploit opportunities for the acquisition of personal wealth.

In this respect, there is an important difference between the traditional and New Right perspectives on property. The traditional conservative argument in favour of private property is more closely related to *social status*. The New Right argument, on the other hand, is less determined by considerations of social rank or status, or the responsibilities that flow from higher status. In this respect, New Right conservatism is (paradoxically) more egalitarian than traditional conservatism. For New Right theorists, anyone can, theoretically, own property. Private ownership gives individuals a 'stake' in society. Once they have acquired property, they can acquire other forms of capital such as private education for their children and other expressions of social power.

Perhaps the best example of this outlook is Margaret Thatcher's defence of home ownership, a centrepiece of Conservative Party policy in the 1980s. Frustrated by their lowly status as 'council tenants', many aspirational working-class voters came to believe that becoming a leaseholder would allow them greater wealth, status and opportunities. In this they were encouraged by the government, and for many individuals the policy was beneficial. However, in accordance with market-libertarian principles, very little help was offered to those who struggled to finance their debts once the cost of borrowing increased and the value of their homes decreased in the early 1990s, leading to repossession and personal ruin for many.

What are the main economic and political reasons for the rise of the New Right?

This philosophical perspective, albeit in a less extreme form, underlies the entire project of the New Right. However, the revival of conservative political fortunes must also be seen as a response to more practical problems of economic organisation — problems that emerged as the era of postwar growth and prosperity drew to a close in the 1970s. The tendencies of the capitalist system towards periodic economic crises, and the threat of disorder arising from political polarisation, led reform-oriented conservative economists and politicians to question the wisdom of the postwar social-democratic consensus.

In this way, the rise of the New Right can be seen as a response to the crisis of hegemony in the social-democratic systems of the West. This resulted in the realignment of conservatism in the 1980s as an ideology concerned primarily with the defence of market capitalism.

Economic decline

The spectre of economic stagnation was a key feature of political debate in the 1970s. The postwar recovery and the prosperity of the 1950s and 1960s gave way to a decline in the traditional manufacturing sector and a rise in trade union militancy. This led many conservatives to question whether the Keynesian policy of managed capitalism — based on increased public spending and full employment — was really viable.

One of the first Tory politicians to raise the issue was Enoch Powell (1912–98), who believed that the ideology of managed capitalism was the principal barrier to economic growth. Powell argued that a new form of economic discipline was required, based on a withdrawal of the state from the market and the abandonment of fiscal policy as a lever of economic control (monetarism). Like the Chicago economist Milton Friedman, Powell believed that the real enemy of economic progress was not unemployment but inflation, which Keynesian policies had failed to resolve.

The initial appeal of monetarism within the Conservative Party was limited to a handful of right-wing ideologues who objected to the collectivist tendencies in social democracy. Inspired by the work of Hayek and Friedman, conservatives such as Keith Joseph and Samuel Brittan began to argue that the best way of dealing with loss-making industries and recalcitrant trade unions was to allow unemployment to find its 'natural' level. If the power of labour to negotiate inflationary wage increments were weakened, the market could exert a form of discipline which, in tandem with a liberalisation of global trade, would have positive consequences for business and finance.

The formula advocated by monetarists appeared deceptively simple: price stability and a stable balance of payments can be achieved if governments restrict the money supply and allow exchange rates to fluctuate. In political terms, however, this reduced economic management implied a break with the social-democratic consensus that had determined the parameters of political

decision making since 1945. To engineer such a radical transition, it was necessary to portray social democracy itself as a historic but failed compromise between capitalism and socialism — one that was increasingly unsuited to the changing needs of a global economy.

Political crisis

Conservative politicians believed that the policies of Edward Heath's government (1970–74) had been a failure because they did not tackle the problem of 'managed decline'. Unlike the intellectuals of the New Right, Edward Heath was committed to middle-way paternalistic conservatism, but his attempts to deal with and appease the left were unsuccessful. This created an opening for a group of determined individuals around Margaret Thatcher, who instinctively rejected compromise in favour of confrontation.

The political problems of the 1970s are often depicted as a crisis of legitimacy in the capitalist system, exacerbated by the growth of left-wing radicalism among workers, students and other opposition groups. A popular view in the works of conservative thinkers was the idea of an 'ungovernability crisis', brought about by disillusionment with the failure of governments to satisfy the rising expectations of key groups for state action.

The logic of this phenomenon was straightforward: the more the state intervenes to determine social outcomes and the more the public expects state intervention to resolve economic and social problems, the weaker the state in fact becomes in fulfilling its primary functions, namely:

- preserving public order
- defending private property
- enforcing contractual obligations

This idea was popularised by conservative intellectuals and politicians such as Anthony King, Samuel Brittan and Norman St John-Stevas, whose work reflects the deep misgivings within right-wing circles about the expansion of democratic freedoms, the emergence of extra-parliamentary social movements, the growth of coercive special interests and the inflation of contradictory social expectations for equality and prosperity.

As Samuel Brittan (1975) argued, excessive expectations of state action risked undermining the fragile social order upon which market society is based. Trade unions, in particular, habitually used coercive tactics to achieve economic goals, forcing employers to turn to the state to resolve industrial disputes, and often achieving inflationary wage increases, which in turn further inflate expectations of benefits to follow.

The view that the UK was in the midst of an ungovernability crisis took hold among key sections of the Conservative Party, who ousted Heath in favour of Thatcher in 1975. The new party leader appeared to offer a more decisive alternative to the middle-way conservative ideology of Tory paternalism, and her election victory in 1979 represented a turning point in postwar history. Although Thatcher was driven as much by a traditional preference for prudence and hard work as by the technical virtues of monetarist theory, her strident defence of macroeconomic stability and balanced budgets convinced the voters to give her a mandate to introduce the political measures necessary to sell off the UK's loss-making industries, to deregulate the financial system, and to confront trade union militancy.

The ascendance of the New Right did not bring about an immediate end to the political crisis of the UK state. Unlike the military regime in Chile — the first country to experiment with monetarist policies — Thatcher's government could not simply eliminate those opposed to neoliberal reforms. Like Chile, however, there was opposition on the left (and rather more muted opposition within the Conservative Party itself) to the monetarist agenda. Critics feared that the government's openly hostile approach to industrial relations could increase political polarisation, and many Tories feared that Thatcher would have to retreat from her controversial proposals if she did not succeed in generating a consensus for change.

Yet as Andrew Gamble argues, the critics underestimated Thatcher's political determination and ideological resolve. He argues that:

> The alliance that was formed under the Thatcher leadership between the populists and the ideologues in the Conservative Party proved a powerful one. It allowed the New Right project to become installed as a framework within which thinking about policy could go ahead. It was accepted that to reverse Britain's relative economic decline, a major break with postwar social democracy and its attendant ideologies and doctrines, such as Keynesianism, had to be carried through. It was a vision of a new social order and the faith that it could be brought about, which sustained the New Right and made the Thatcher government appear radical even when its actions were cautious.
>
> Andrew Gamble, 'The political economy of freedom' (1986)

A key feature of the Thatcher period in UK politics was the increasing decisional autonomy of the core executive, which may be seen as a response to the long-term dual crisis of the UK state. Bob Jessop and others (1988) have argued that this dual crisis stemmed from two sources:

- the institutional weakness of the parliamentary system, which fails to provide adequate democratic consultation
- the weakness of interest representation, which fails to coordinate and reconcile competing social and economic interests

The long-term structural crisis of the British state, brought about by the decline of the old tripartite system — in which the state acted to reconcile conflicts between industry and the trade unions, encouraged the Conservatives to seek non-bureaucratic solutions to the problems of political organisation without relinquishing the highly centralised power of Whitehall. The main consequence of this was the development of Thatcherism as a quasi-presidential regime based on the paradoxical idea of using state power to 'roll back the frontiers of the state'.

What do New Right conservatives mean by 'rolling back the frontiers of the state'?

The idea of 'rolling back the state' is based on a neoliberal assumption that *the government which governs least governs best*. New Right conservatism stands above all for the belief that the state should not be involved in the determination of social outcomes, and that individuals should, to the greatest extent possible, be allowed control over their own property. This suggests a commitment to economic liberalism, and presupposes a tacit if not explicit consensus within the educated and commercial classes that accumulation is a legitimate pursuit, and that the proper function of the state is to provide a stable legal and political framework within which private accumulation can take place.

As Eric Evans comments, this entails an attack on the government ethic itself, and on the assumption that state bureaucracies have a legitimate right to monopolise the provision of public services such as education, health, housing and social welfare. Although conservatives such as Margaret Thatcher have been ruthless in using the coercive power of the state against their enemies — exemplified by the abolition of six Labour-controlled metropolitan councils in 1985 on the basis that these left-wing city councils had become like a 'state within a state' (Evans 1997) — the assault on the authority and prerogative power of the public sector is a key feature of New Right political strategy, which has also continued under New Labour.

However, there is a certain irony in the New Right idea of using the power of the state to demarcate the proper limits of state intervention. How can politicians utilise the apparatus of the state in such a way as to reverse the growth of the state as a centralised political authority? Is the growth of the centralised administrative apparatus of the state not an irreversible feature of modernity?

Or can the activities of the state be curtailed by restricting the idea of what the state should or should not legitimately do?

To understand the rhetoric of 'rolling back the frontiers of the state', we need to examine briefly the logic behind the growth of the modern state. As James Arnt Aune (2002) argues, libertarians such as Murray Rothbard are critical of liberal and socialist intellectuals for promoting the idea of the 'benevolent state', and for providing the intellectual manpower to staff government bureaucracies. In this respect, right-wing libertarians share common cause with traditional conservatives, who argue that left-wing intellectuals popularise ideologies which only serve to justify the dangerous extension of state authority and the expansion of the public sector.

It is this problem that most exercised New Right politicians in the 1980s, particularly in the UK and the USA, where the neoliberal assault on the institutions of 'big government' found its fullest expression.

The emergence of a New Right agenda

The development of an anti-state agenda within the New Right follows a clear and definite logic, which attempts to unify the neoliberal and neoconservative strands of modern conservative ideology into a coherent political programme. This anti-state agenda is fuelled by opposition to the growth of state power in the West, as exemplified by the Keynesian welfare state in the UK since 1945 and the expansion of the US federal government under the New Deal.

Political sociologists agree that the growth of centralised states based on a monopolisation of the means of coercion is a central feature of modernity. A basic pattern of state expansion takes place, which can be summarised as follows:

- By gradually co-opting and replacing naturally evolving social institutions, the centralised apparatus of the state expands its role and function in civil society, becoming effectively indispensable.
- In addition to basic provisions such as defence and policing, governments also provide education, healthcare, transportation, welfare and housing — all of which must be paid for through tax revenue.
- Although there are limits to the viability of state intervention (for example, the socialisation and care of children is a core function of the family), since 1945 Western governments have expanded the range of areas in which the state is legitimately involved in the organisation of social life.

The development of the modern centralised state in the postwar era is primarily the result of the institutionalisation of social expectations within the

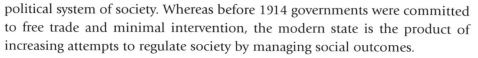

political system of society. Whereas before 1914 governments were committed to free trade and minimal intervention, the modern state is the product of increasing attempts to regulate society by managing social outcomes.

The first tentative steps in this direction were taken in the 1930s in response to the Great Depression, which threatened political instability. However, the real turning point came during the Second World War, when a large part of UK manufacturing and distribution was placed under state control. The Labour politicians charged with running the war economy made a virtue of necessity in the postwar era by legally nationalising what were, in effect, already state-run concerns. This created the basis for the postwar mixed economy, based on:

- managed growth
- low unemployment
- fixed exchange rates
- expansion of welfare

For New Right conservatives, however, this expansion of government is unacceptable, not only because social democracy inflates popular expectations of state action (thereby making the business of government more difficult), but also because the state is *less efficient* at allocating social goods and services. Pointing to the achievements of the great Victorian entrepreneurs, whose enterprise and industry were viewed as key sources of economic progress in the nineteenth century, New Right conservatives emphasise the contradiction of socialism, which encourages people to believe that the state is the best means for organising a just distribution of resources.

It is this belief that motivated Conservatives in the UK and Republicans in the USA to attempt to reduce expectations of state intervention by limiting the range of economic activities performed by government, thereby 'rolling back' the frontiers of the state. Following election victories in 1979 and 1980 respectively, both Margaret Thatcher and US president Ronald Reagan set in motion a series of reforms designed to introduce what Samuel Brittan describes as a 'tough-minded, business-oriented, stand-on-your-own-two-feet brand of conservatism' (Brittan 1973).

For conservatives on both sides of the Atlantic, the goal was to legitimise a radical economic agenda that would appeal to a cross-section of voters, based on a return to laissez-faire capitalism and the deregulation of trade and commerce.:

- Thatcherism' and 'Reaganomics' shared a common economic objective, namely, the *delegitimisation* of social democracy (or what US conservatives refer to as 'vital centre liberalism').
- From a neoconservative perspective, however, they were also both hostile to the social revolution of the 1960s, which was blamed for the perceived decline of traditional social authority and the 'destructive' growth of egalitarianism.

To what extent is New Right conservatism simply a defence of free-market capitalism?

For some observers, the tension between the neoliberal and neoconservative aspects of New Right policies is evidence of a fundamental contradiction in the philosophical–ideological basis of New Right thought. For others, this apparent contradiction is less problematic. They argue that the economic and social agendas of New Right thought are mutually reinforcing, and that far from being contradictory the demand for decreased state intervention is perfectly compatible with the demand for a reassertion of social authority.

Market libertarianism

In his classic study, *The Free Economy and the Strong State* (1988), Andrew Gamble argues that it is possible to approach the political strategy of the New Right in three ways:

- as a hegemonic strategy, designed to overturn the social-democratic/liberal-welfarist consensus that predominated in Europe and the USA during the postwar era
- as an accumulation strategy, designed to advance business interests by increasing the power of capital over labour
- as a form of statecraft, reflecting the traditional conservative preoccupation with winning elections and controlling the levers of state power

Although there is a tension between its celebration of materialism and individualism on the one hand and its reassertion of traditionalism on the other, New Right conservatism is indisputably oriented towards the promotion of business interests. The real question is: *to what extent does this defence of business interests conflict with the traditional basis of conservatism?*

As a hegemonic strategy, New Right ideology is opposed to the 'compromise ideology' of middle-way conservatism, with its emphasis on pragmatism, stability and social cohesion. For New Right leaders, the idea that conservatives should accommodate themselves to a discredited model of economic management was absurd: the target of conservative policy should be to eliminate the vestiges of state socialism. Politicians are not being radical by breaking with established methods if those methods do not deliver the goods; it is simply common sense.

This idea was expressed by Margaret Thatcher using the analogy of 'good housekeeping': *the prudent housewife is the one who refuses to spend what has not been earned*. In this sense Thatcherism can be seen as a latter-day form of Whiggism, which challenged the complacent Toryism of one-nation conservatives. Rather than being a pragmatic form of statecraft, oriented exclusively towards the perpetuation of Conservative rule, Thatcher grasped the opportunity for change by exploiting the collapse of the Callaghan government in 1978–79 to introduce policies that Heath had failed to implement.

The main economic policies of the New Right can be summarised as follows:

- *Defence of economic liberty*. Freedom is defined in economic terms as the freedom to accumulate wealth and to exercise consumer choice.
- *Reduction of state intervention*. There is no place for the 'state as collective capitalist' philosophy, which characterises socialist theory.
- *Deregulation*. It is the duty of the state to provide a legal framework for accumulation by allowing unrestricted trade and commerce.
- *Anti-welfarism*. State aid should be made strictly conditional on real need, in order to reduce the debilitating consequences of welfare dependency.
- *Reduction of the public sector*. Both the size and cost of the public sector should be reduced in order to limit the expansion of government into more areas of life.

However, the rise of the New Right also represented a chance to reassert the traditional social power of business and finance in a way that could not have been anticipated — and which certainly would not have been possible — a decade earlier. The reasons for this lie not only in the declining appeal of parliamentary socialism in the advanced countries of the West, but in the worldwide decline of state socialism as an alternative form of industrial organisation. In the early 1970s socialism still seemed plausible to many mainstream voters; by the mid-1980s, however, with the Soviet Union a declining power, fewer people were prepared to accept the idea that state intervention is the best means for dealing with the problems of economic decline.

In the USA, the delegitimisation of the liberal-welfarist model was even more pronounced than in the UK. The goal of the Thatcher administration was to arrest the problem of decline, by discrediting socialism as an inefficient system for organising a modern economy in which the consumer rather than the producer is the priority. In the USA, by contrast, where socialists have never enjoyed widespread support, the aim of the right was to discredit liberal welfarism by reasserting the 'end of ideology' thesis.

This thesis was introduced by the Harvard sociologist Daniel Bell in the 1960s, and was subsequently developed by the political economist Francis Fukuyama, who coined the term the 'end of history' to signify the exhaustion of emancipatory ideological thinking in the wake of the collapse of communism. According to this view, capitalism is the only viable means of guaranteeing social prosperity and innovation. Other ideologies have attempted to challenge the hegemonic values of the capitalist system, but they have all been found wanting because they are inconsistent with human nature.

This reflects a non-secular tendency in US political culture to seek a final and definitive *modus operandi*, negating the search for new forms of social and economic organisation by 'resetting the historical clock' to a time before the New Deal. Whereas 'vital centre liberals' such as John F. Kennedy tried to make US society more inclusive and just, New Right politicians were responding to conservative demands to arrest the pace of emancipation by restricting the capacity of the state to address the social consequences of economic, racial and gender inequality.

Possessive individualism

In this respect, libertarianism does indeed find common cause with conservatism in New Right ideology by reasserting the principle of possessive individualism. According to C. B. Macpherson (1962), the ideology of possessive individualism has its roots in eighteenth-century liberal political and economic theory, particularly the ideas of John Locke and his followers.

This ideology reflects an overriding belief (discussed above) in the importance of private property as the *material basis of individualism and economic freedom*. In contrast to socialism, which posits community and cooperation as the principles of social organisation, possessive individualism reaffirms the validity of the economic agent as the sovereign individual of capitalism. All individuals should take full personal responsibility for their own material welfare and security, rather than rely on the community or the state as a source of sustenance.

The possessive market model reiterates Thomas Hobbes's preference for a society in which each individual has full control over his or her property and labour, and exists in a state of perpetual competition with other 'sovereign individuals'. Macpherson summarises this point as follows:

> Whatever the degree of state action, the possessive market model permits individuals who want more…than they have to seek to convert the natural powers of other men to their use. They do so through the market, in which everyone is necessarily involved. Since the market is continually competitive, those who would be content with the level of satisfaction they have are compelled to fresh exertions by every attempt of the others to increase theirs. Those who would be content with the level they have cannot keep it without seeking more power, that is, without seeking to transfer more powers of others to themselves, to compensate for the increasing amount that the competitive efforts of others are transferring from them.

Authoritarian populism

In the 1980s, the ideology of possessive individualism found expression in the New Right assault on the principles of community and cooperation, and in the reassertion of state authority as a means of defending the security of the market. To its supporters, New Right conservatism was seen as the optimal means of addressing the problems of economic decline within the context of a strong state. Stuart Hall (1983) suggests that the origins of authoritarian populism lie in a convergence between:

- the demands of the economic ruling class, which wanted to discipline the workforce and increase capital accumulation, and
- the demands of middle-class and lower middle-class strata, which wanted the state to act against the 'forces of disorder', whom Thatcher herself famously labelled 'the enemy within'

Hall has been criticised for overemphasising the coherence of the postwar social-democratic consensus prior to 1979, which obscures the drift towards a law and order state under the 1976–79 Labour government. Nevertheless, as Gamble argues, the New Right deemed the idea of a coercive, disciplinary state necessary for the following reasons:

- to reduce the size of the public sector and the level of state intervention in the economy
- to police the new market order
- to make the economy more efficient
- to reassert traditional forms of social and political authority

Gamble (1988) argues that the political logic of the free economy and strong state lies in the use of coercive state power as a means of defeating and containing those vested interests that threaten to disrupt the operation of the free market economy. 'If the state makes the protection of those institutions of the free economy its priority', he argues, 'then it creates the basis of its own legitimacy'.

Although there is a risk that the civil liberties of private individuals might be jeopardised in defence of economic liberty (for example, in the use of surveillance against subversive groups), New Right conservatives justify the extension of state power as a necessary condition of economic liberty. As such, the New Right defence of freedom represents a commitment to the legitimate power of capital as the basis of social order.

In practical terms, this amounts to an appeal to economic independence and private accumulation as the primary virtues of self-respecting, disciplined individuals who represent the primary source of wealth creation in society, and who therefore deserve to enjoy the full protection of the law. As Ruth Levitas (1986) concludes:

> This concern of the authoritarian right with internal subversion runs alongside a concern with law and order, and this too provides an ambiguous point of linkage with the neo-liberal position. Although this is not a dominant theme for free-marketeers except in relation to trade union activities, they do manifest a strong reliance upon the law — as enshrined in the judiciary and civil courts, rather than in overt policing.

In this respect, neoliberal New Right conservatives are more concerned with the procedural status of law as a means of policing the market and defending property rights, whereas neoconservatives are more concerned with reasserting traditional forms of authority and allegiance as desirable phenomena in themselves. The two approaches are, on the one hand, *compatible* in their defence of self-interest and social inequality. There is, after all, a close connection between social authority and economic influence, given that economic power is a precondition for social status in possessive market societies. On the other hand, they are *distinct* and *potentially* contradictory in their differential adherence to authority and tradition as necessary and desirable features of social order.

To what extent, therefore, is New Right conservatism simply a defence of the free market? The evidence seems to suggest three important facts about New Right ideology, in the following order of importance. First, the philosophical essence of New Right conservatism lies in its radical defence of property freedom. Philosophers such as Nozick and Hayek developed a powerful critique of egalitarian theories of society based on a just distribution of resources. New Right politicians adapted this critique to legitimise a return to the principles of economic laissez faire: in particular, the view that the market is the best means of allocating resources.

A second important feature of New Right ideology is its assault on the Keynesian welfare state. New Right theorists opposed the idea that the state should be involved in economic decision making, especially through the use of fiscal policy (taxes). The key economic goal should be macroeconomic stability rather than reducing unemployment, which helps to promote labour discipline by encouraging workers to adapt to the changing needs of the market.

A third important feature is its sustained critique of the permissive society that emerged in the 1960s and 1970s as a result of increasing affluence and individualism. The moral dimension of neoconservative New Right ideology has been less successful than the neoliberal critique of social democracy,

A gathering in Hyde Park, London — all part of the 'permissive' 1960s

although both neoliberals and neoconservatives share the view that welfare dependence has a corrupting influence on individual self-reliance and personal responsibility.

Conclusion

In this chapter we have analysed in depth both the ideological origins and the political–economic logic of the rise of the New Right. The revival of conservatism in the UK and the USA can be traced back to dissatisfaction with the postwar social-democratic consensus based on an expansion in the size of the state and its role in economic decision making. From an intellectual perspective, the hegemonic strategy of the New Right owes much to the ideas of libertarian and neoconservative theorists who, in their different ways, set out to draw attention to the perceived weakness of *social democracy* as a system of economic management, and the perceived weakness of *liberalism* as a means of regulating and sustaining social consensus.

As we shall see in the final chapter, there is evidence to suggest that the neoconservative agenda of the New Right has been rather *less* successful than its neoliberal agenda (particularly in the UK, where there is no sizeable 'moral majority' to compare with the USA's Christian Coalition). This is because the main effect of the New Right has been to discredit the conventional idea of welfare capitalism, according to which the state should play an ever greater role in allocating resources. The moral agenda of neoconservatism appeals to communitarians and traditionalists disillusioned with liberal individualism. But market libertarianism — despite its disruptive impact on social stability, authority and tradition — remains the key policy objective of New Right political movements, seeking to adjust economic policies to the changing needs of the global market.

In Chapter 5, we will examine in greater detail the ideological character and political–sociological basis of modern conservatism, and attempt to determine whether or not the free market ideology of the New Right can in fact be described as 'conservative' at all. On closer examination, the rise of the New Right in the 1980s has been responsible for a deeper transformation of the Conservative Party, from Tory paternalism to a more individualistic, 'Whiggish' liberalism. This Hayekian conservatism retains a strong preference for the defence of authority, patriotism and tradition, although even these core conservative ideals are in many ways subordinate to the more fundamental defence of free-market capitalism.

Task 4.1

Using a copy of the following diagram, outline four policy ideas associated with market libertarianism.

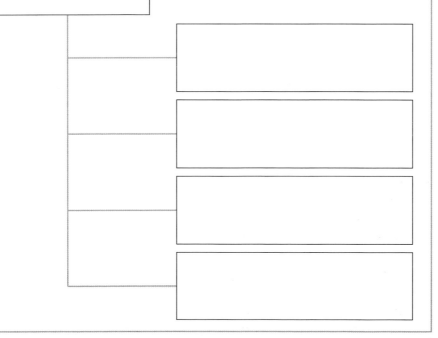

The logic of market liberalism

Task 4.1 (continued)

Guidance

Neoliberalism is concerned with freeing the economy from political controls and reducing the constraints on business to accumulate profits. We often refer to neoliberalism as 'market libertarianism', which asserts that individual liberty can only be guaranteed if people are free to accumulate wealth and dispose of their property as they see fit.

Four key areas of concern from neoliberals are: reduced taxation, reduced public expenditure, macroeconomic stability (low inflation) and a deregulated marketplace (elimination of state controls on business activity). Using the arguments contained in the chapter, explain briefly in the diagram why these are considered fundamental.

Task 4.2

Read Source A and complete the questions that follow.

Source A

[New Right theorists] point out that the pursuit of equality of outcome leads to stagnation, injustice and, ultimately, tyranny. Stagnation results from the fact that social 'levelling' serves to cap aspirations and remove incentives for enterprise and hard work. To the extent that a society moves towards the goal
5 of social equality it will therefore pay a heavy price in terms of sterility and inertia. The economic cost of equality is, however, less forbidding than the moral price to be paid. This is a lesson which New Right thinkers such as Friedrich Hayek and Keith Joseph were at pains to teach. In their view the socialist principle of equality is based on little more than social envy, the
10 desire to have what the wealthy already possess. Policies that aim to promote equality by redistributing wealth do little more than rob the rich in order to pay the poor. The simple fact is, Hayek argued, that people are very different, they have different aspirations, talents, dispositions and so forth, and to treat them as equals must therefore result in inequality.

Andrew Heywood, *Political Theory: An Introduction* (1999)

(a) What is meant by 'social "levelling"' (line 3)?

(b) Why do New Right theorists stress the negative economic effects of social levelling?

(c) Why do New Right theorists suggest that the socialist principle of egalitarianism is based on envy (line 9)? Is this fair?

(d) How might paternalistic conservatives differ from New Right conservatives in their view of the morality of redistribution? Is the redistribution of wealth wholly illegitimate?

Task 4.2 (continued)

Guidance

Remember that the main thrust of the New Right critique is against egalitarianism and collectivism, which are the core components of socialist ideologies. New Right theorists believe that socialism undermines the incentives that individuals have to compete.

For New Right theorists, the idea that the state has a right to determine economic outcomes is both economically and morally misguided. It is economically misguided because its reduces enterprise; it is morally misguided because, by treating people as equals in an abstract way, it ignores the special talents that some people have, which give them a legitimate right to earn or possess more than those who do not have such talents.

Useful websites

- On the conservative idea of liberty and economic freedom, see:
  http://acuf.org/principles/p_freedom.asp
- For a critical view of libertarian conservatism, see:
  www.banned-books.com/galambos/conservatism.html

Further reading

- Aune, J. A. (2002) *Selling the Free Market*, The Guildford Press.
- Brittan, S. (1973) *Capitalism and the Permissive Society*, Macmillan.
- Brittan, S. (1975) 'The economic contradictions of democracy' in *British Journal of Political Science* No. 5.
- Evans, E. J. (1997) *Thatcher and Thatcherism*, Routledge.
- Gamble, A. (1986) 'The political economy of freedom', in R. Levitas (ed.) *The Ideology of the New Right*, Polity Press.
- Gamble, A. (1988) *The Free Economy and the Strong State: The Politics of Thatcherism*, Macmillan.
- Hall, S. (1983) 'The great moving right show' in S. Hall and M. Jacques (eds.) (1983) *The Politics of Thatcherism*, Lawrence and Wishart.
- Jessop, B. et al. (1988) *Thatcherism: a Tale of Two Nations*, Polity Press.
- Levitas, R. (1986) 'Competition and compliance', in R. Levitas (ed.) *The Ideology of the New Right*, Polity Press.
- Macpherson, C. B. (1962) *The Political Theory of Possessive Individualism*, Clarendon Press.
- Nozick, R. (1974) *Anarchy, State and Utopia*, Basic Books Inc.

Is the Conservative Party in the UK still 'conservative'?

Introduction

A key theme of this book has been the distinction between traditional paternalistic conservatism and modern New Right conservatism. This distinction can be theorised in many ways: as a *historical* division reflecting the difference between conservatism in the nineteenth and twentieth centuries; as an *ideological* division reflecting two different views of the individual; or as a *political* division, reflecting two radically different responses to the challenge of socialism.

In this final chapter, our primary aim will be to assess whether the Conservative Party is still a conservative political movement based on a recognisably 'conservative' ideology. This may seem an odd question. *Of course* the Tories are conservative: their policies reflect a typically conservative brand of economic prudence, patriotism and respect for traditional institutions. However, in dealing with the political character of modern conservatism in the UK, students must be able to assess whether the defence of market libertarianism at the heart of modern conservatism represents an authentic revision of conservative ideology or whether modern conservatism represents the pursuit of economic liberalism by other means.

UK politics entered a new era in the 1980s, leading to the emergence of a new post-socialist liberal-democratic consensus. This consensus has been built on the hegemonic view that social-democratic systems of economic management are no longer viable in a world dominated by *global* market forces. As the political theorist Jacques Rancière argues (1999), developed capitalist societies have now reached a new stage of 'consensual post-democracy': what matters is not adversarial party politics as such, but a consensual ideological legitimation of the marketplace society.

Any party that hopes to conquer the centre ground in UK politics must adapt to the formula of:

- macrobudgetary stability
- the economic discipline of the market
- intergovernmental cooperation on cross-border issues such as environmentalism and trade

Although governments may resort to sovereign state intervention under exceptional circumstances (for example, to defend the national currency during times of crisis), unless parties can adapt to the new orthodoxy they will remain, effectively, unelectable.

In the UK, the transition to a modern consensus-based system began with a dealignment of class voting patterns in the 1970s and early 1980s, which gave the Tories an electoral advantage over Labour. Under Margaret Thatcher, the Conservatives relentlessly pursued a neoliberal economic agenda that placed the risk-taking individual at the heart of its political philosophy. This hegemonic strategy was eventually adopted and adapted by Labour under the leadership of Tony Blair, whose intuitive and skilful reading of the post-socialist ideological environment allowed New Labour to capitalise on the split within the Conservative Party in the mid-1990s. Following the Thatcherite model, New Labour demonstrated the political importance of the new post-socialist consensus, although the transition from 'old' Labour to New Labour alienated many traditional supporters, who objected to the adoption of middle-class values such as self-betterment, thrift and competition.

Tony Blair: architect of Labour's ideological turn

Like New Labour, however, the Conservative Party has evolved in recent decades in a way that displays both continuity and discontinuity.

- On the one hand, the Tories are clearly still the party of the right in the UK. They have survived as the natural home of the business and professional classes, and (despite divisions over Europe in the 1990s) of 'patriotic' voters (upper class, middle class and chauvinistic working class). From this perspective, the Tories are still the party most committed to defence of the Union (particularly in relation to the transfer of sovereignty to the EU) and to defence of the pound as the national currency.
- On the other hand, the Conservative Party is clearly *no longer* the party of old-fashioned paternalistic Tories such as Winston Churchill and Harold

Macmillan. The revival of the party's fortunes in the 1980s was based on a hegemonic strategy aimed at abolishing the old tripartite system, reasserting the power of business and dismantling the Keynesian welfare state. This agenda was pursued ruthlessly and with notably less concern for the negative social consequences of economic liberalisation.

In order to answer the question posed at the start of this chapter, therefore, it is necessary to examine:
- the political and ideological character of Thatcherism, and
- the extent to which the Conservative Party has relinquished its traditional identity as a broad, nationally based coalition of the centre-right

Although the Tories are still the natural home for those voters whom Ken Clarke famously described as the 'solid citizens of middle England', there is evidence to suggest that New Labour's shift to the ideological centre of UK politics has robbed the Tories of their traditional majority. Added to this is the demographic weakness of the Tory vote in the urban UK, as younger middle-class voters have deserted the party in favour of New Labour and the Liberal Democrats.

Having laid the basis for a new form of consensus politics in the 1980s, therefore, the Conservative Party is now struggling to redefine itself as a more tolerant, liberal, post-Thatcherite party in tune with both traditional older voters and younger cosmopolitan voters. This political 'rebranding' in many respects completes the party's transition from Tory paternalism to Whiggish liberalism, based on a pragmatic adaptation to the changing political logic of the liberal–capitalist system.

In what sense is Thatcherism a two-nation ideology?

The Conservatives have traditionally portrayed themselves as the 'natural party of government' in the UK, uniting a cross-section of commercial and professional interests behind a pragmatic defence of middle-class values and concerns. Yet it would be a mistake to underestimate the *radicalism* of modern political conservatism in the UK. Clearly, some observers have exaggerated the radical nature of the Thatcher governments — particularly her first administration between 1979 and 1983. But there is no doubt that 1979 represents a watershed in UK political history, signalling not only the end of the postwar social-democratic consensus, but also the increasing polarisation of UK society between winners and losers in the new enterprise economy.

Realignment and dealignment

It has been suggested that the revival of conservatism in the 1980s can be traced back to a process of class realignment, whereby the Conservatives successfully won over a new constituency of disillusioned Labour voters (so-called 'working class Tories'). It is certainly true that a significant number of skilled workers deserted Labour in 1979, fearing for their own futures in a country troubled by industrial unrest and fears of decline. Allied to this was an anxiety that Labour was powerless to control radical trade unions affiliated to the party, which exercised a power of veto over new policy initiatives.

However, a more convincing explanation is that the rise of the New Right in the 1980s was the product of a dealignment in class voting patterns, as a result of which Tories successfully established a broad base of political support across the social classes, ensuring the party a natural majority in parliament. This allowed the Conservatives to become the 'dominant party' in the UK political system — a position subsequently relinquished by New Labour following Tony Blair's accession as party leader.

Nevertheless, the key question remains: *how could the Tories have benefited from this class dealignment if the central ideological message of the party was based on a reassertion of business interests and middle-class values?* How, in other words, could Margaret Thatcher, and her allies in Fleet Street and the City, present the Tories as a populist alternative among a cross-section of voters if the Conservatives depicted themselves as an unapologetic party of the right?

The answer to this puzzle lies in a peculiar feature of Thatcherism: namely, its divisiveness. In pluralist societies, politics is a competitive struggle between interests, in which groups attempt to monopolise resources for themselves, or at least to deny access to such resources among their opponents. By encouraging voters to see beyond local and class-based allegiances, Thatcher managed to recruit a large number of supporters frustrated by the apparent failure of adversarial politics, which seemed to result in a submergence of important issues at election time and the reversal of initiatives in the face of opposition from vested interests.

The development of a two-nation ideology

The essential innovation of Thatcherism was to present itself as anti-elitist, as a non-class-specific defence of common sense and social respectability. In this sense, Thatcherism represents a populist transition from an inclusive one-nation ideology to the rhetoric of two nations. Whereas Tory paternalists had traditionally defended the one-nation ideal as a means of integrating middle-class and lower middle-class voters behind the goals of the ruling establishment

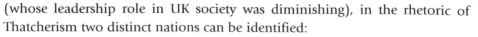
(whose leadership role in UK society was diminishing), in the rhetoric of Thatcherism two distinct nations can be identified:

- a nation of respectable citizens in employment and hard-working families of independent means
- a subordinate nation of non-skilled workers, non-English minorities, the unemployed and the socially excluded

This idea is captured well by Bob Jessop (1988), who argues that Thatcherism entails an explicit rejection of the Keynesian welfare state in favour of a two-nation ideology. Thatcherism, he explains, is:

> concerned with managing the political repercussions of an 'underclass' whose existence is taken for granted rather than seen as a rebuke to the nation's conscience. Indeed it is happy to expand the underclass of the unemployed new waged poor to stimulate the purgative effects of economic crisis. It also intends to cut an allegedly overgrown welfare state and to construct a minimal, selective, 'social security' state akin to that of the United States. …In terms of the politics of support, the 'two nations' approach requires that the productive be rewarded through the market for their contribution to production; conversely the parasitic must suffer for their failure to contribute adequately to the market.

Although this view has been challenged by those who defend the 'trickle-down' theory of increasing prosperity (where the wealth accumulation of advantaged groups is gradually dispersed throughout society, indirectly benefiting disadvantaged groups), the widening gap between rich and poor in the UK since 1979 indicates that the two-nation model is not entirely inaccurate.

Surveys such as the government's own *Social Trends* research and the *Family Expenditure Survey* reveal that the burden of increased indirect taxation has been felt more acutely by the poorest sections of the population since the 1980s. The shift from progressive taxation to indirect taxes on utilities and consumer goods means that poorer families pay a disproportionate amount of their income in tax compared to the wealthier sections of society. This trend has accelerated under New Labour, which has preserved the income tax rates introduced by the Thatcher governments of the 1980s.

Homelessness in Britain: self-inflicted poverty or a consequence of Conservative policies?

Social exclusion

In ideological terms, however, it is the overall emphasis of the New Right which indicates a marked shift in conservatism from the rhetoric of social inclusion to the rhetoric of social exclusion.

This rhetorical shift is reflected in the tendency of New Right conservatives to deny the relevance of society as a cohesive association of individuals united by common identity and mutual dependence. In place of the traditional conservative preference for an 'organic society', New Right conservatives privilege competitive exchange as the primary form and basis of social interaction. According to this view, the coexistence of individuals is dependent less on naturally occurring emotional bonds between individuals and communities than on their relative status within the division of labour, and their contribution to the generation of national wealth.

For this reason, New Right politicians such as Norman Tebbit and Keith Joseph were quick to emphasise the economic dimension of social mobility: in Tebbit's famous phrase, those negatively affected by the market (or by policies aimed at revitalising the market) should stop complaining and get 'on their bikes' to find alternative employment.

Although Tebbit's views aroused indignation on the left (and concern among Tory 'wets' sceptical of Thatcher's radical agenda), at the heart of his argument lay a blunt recommendation: individuals should cease to depend on the state to help them secure a livelihood and should seize the opportunities presented by the new 'enterprise culture'. Failure to adapt to the economic discipline of the market (even where failure could be attributed to undeserved social disadvantage) was viewed as evidence of the negative consequences of welfare dependence, which encourages people to believe that the 'world owes them a living'.

To what extent is there a tension between economic freedom and social stability in modern conservatism?

The transition of the Conservative Party from paternalistic Toryism to liberal Whiggism reflects, as we have seen, a deeper shift away from protectionism and social inclusion towards liberalisation and social exclusion. As Ruth Levitas (2005) argues, this shift is mirrored still more dramatically in the conversion

of Labour to the virtues of self-enrichment, consumerism and competition, as a result of which the UK remains a deeply divided society.

Whereas New Labour ideology entails a 'social integrationist' approach to society (i.e. one that is concerned with promoting social cohesion under conditions of instability and social disintegration), the new conservatism can be seen as an unstable, yet powerful, mix of liberal economic policies and authoritarian social values. Since the 1980s, these have coalesced into a defence of bourgeois individualism, based on the idea of 'ordered risk taking' in a secure economic environment.

The question is: is modern conservatism a coherent ideological strategy, or is it a contradictory project that sacrifices the conservative preference for social stability in favour of economic freedom? To answer this question, we have to examine in detail the coherent and contradictory dimension of post-Thatcherite conservatism. The argument proposed here is that, despite the claims of apologists for Tory policies, there is clear evidence that the deregulation of market forces and the celebration of individualism and consumerism in modern conservatism undermined the cohesiveness of UK society, accelerating a trend towards social polarisation and exclusion that New Labour has only partially addressed since 1997.

The impact of market forces

Karl Marx (1818–83) observed that one of the most striking things about capitalism is its 'creative destructiveness'. Marx believed that the centuries of economic development prior to the emergence of capitalism could be likened to the 'prehistory' of humankind. Followers of Marx, such as Karl Polanyi (1866–1964), also saw capitalism as the driving force behind the 'great transformation' which radically altered the structure of European society in the eighteenth century, laying the foundations for the modern industrial economies of the West.

Although Marxists argue that capitalist societies will eventually give way to socialism, they accept that this transition (if it is possible at all) will take place only when the advanced capitalist societies have reached a sufficient level of economic and technological development. The point of this argument is that, *even among opponents of capitalism, there is a recognition that progress and emancipation from poverty are dependent on the further development of capitalism as a basis of modern social and economic order.*

Capitalism threatens local traditions and particular ways of life, but neoliberals argue that failure to adapt to market forces is a recipe for economic decline and stagnation: countries that do not adjust to the discipline of the market risk falling behind in the race for growth and prosperity, even though market forces can (in the short to medium term) result in unemployment and hardship for vulnerable groups who lack the skills necessary to compete effectively for new jobs.

For conservatives there is an inevitable problem of ambivalence in relation to the impact of the free market. This can be seen from the following comparisons:

- In the *nineteenth century*, conservatives in Europe reacted with hostility to the demand for liberal free trade policies because these threatened to undermine their interests. The great landowners of England and Prussia attempted to block free trade legislation until pressure for change became irresistible. The logic of their opposition lay not just in the preservation of economic advantage (i.e. protection against cheaper foreign imports), but in a potential loss of political influence and social authority. Amid the decline in importance of the agricultural sector, landowners were forced to forge new alliances with commercial and industrial interests in order to preserve their status, but in the long term the advent of free trade and the commercialisation of agriculture eroded their political power.

- In the *post-1945 era*, conservatives in the UK and western Europe recognised the value of paternalistic policies as a means for promoting social stability, and — despite objections from dyed-in-the-wool opponents of socialism — the mixed economy and the welfare state were tolerated as necessary evils. Rather than risk a return to the social polarisation and political instability of the interwar years, conservatives accepted the new consensus as a means of controlling and regulating the social impact of the market.

- For *modern* New Right conservatives, the commitment to preserving social authority and tradition is potentially at odds with their parallel commitment to free-market capitalism as both the economic basis of social order and the source of perpetual change. The central problem for modern conservatives lies, therefore, in the consequences arising out of the inner contradiction between pragmatism and rationalism in New Right ideology.

Whereas the *traditional* conservativism emphasises a holistic conception of society as an organic entity in which the stability of the whole is dependent on the correct functioning of the multiplicity of constituent parts, *libertarian* conservatism is based on an atomistic view of society as an aggregation of individuals united only by voluntary bonds of exchange. And, whereas Tory pragmatists emphasise the need for social cohesion and economic regulation, economic liberals advocate privatisation and deregulation as solutions to the problem of economic organisation, accepting the fact that *some individuals will always prosper at the expense of others*.

For followers of Thatcher, this tension was dissolved in the rhetoric of 'Victorian values', which sought to anchor economic freedom within an

authoritarian social framework derived from the hierarchical and patriarchal context of nineteenth-century capitalism.

In other words, New Right politicians believed that the impersonal authority and economic discipline of the *market* could be backed up by the firm hand of the *state*, whose function (as we saw in Chapter 4) would be to 'police' the marketplace by increasing the cost of unemployment and criminality for the individual. By encouraging individuals to take responsibility for their own financial security, health and welfare, New Right leaders believed they could create a more self-reliant and self-responsible society.

The problem for the Conservatives was that many individuals lacked the resources to take advantage of the new enterprise culture, while many who attempted to take advantage of the new opportunities for social mobility lacked sufficient capital to survive the economic rollercoaster that characterised the 'boom and bust' economy of the 1980s and early 1990s.

Thatcherism and neoliberalism

The neoliberal economic agenda of the Conservatives was centred on the reduction of public expenditure and state intervention in the economy, as the following examples indicate.

Privatisation of state-owned monopolies

In European countries such as France, the UK and Italy, the government has traditionally played a stabilising role in the organisation of the economy, creating large state-owned monopolies (e.g. car industries such as British Leyland or Renault) which provide(d) secure employment for large numbers of workers and affordable products and services for the consumer.

For the New Right, however, the inefficiency of public sector companies makes them prime targets for cost-cutting measures, either by forcing them to compete with private sector firms or by selling them off to the highest bidder. In the UK in the 1980s, virtually all state-owned industries were sold off, including British Gas, British Telecom and British Steel. This stimulated activity in the markets and promoted share ownership among wider sections of the population. It allowed the Conservatives to portray their policies as consistent with a 'property-owning democracy'.

Deregulation

Another example of market libertarianism is deregulation, which entails the relaxation of legal and institutional constraints on free trade and commerce. In the 1980s, this was exemplified by the so-called Big Bang, when share dealing was deregulated on the London stock market. This encouraged capital investment by providing incentives for people to speculate on the future value of the market. People were encouraged to invest cash in shares which would increase sharply in value, fuel a speculation boom and increase the popular sense of wealth and prosperity among Conservative supporters.

Reduced taxation

A third example of market libertarianism is reduced taxation, which New Right theorists view as essential to the promotion of choice. As a policy, reduced income tax and corporation tax bring together many dimensions of New Right ideology, including a populist preference for allowing individuals to decide how, and on what, to spend their wealth. Reduced taxation also decreases the total proportion of wealth transferred from the private sector to the public sector — a key policy demand of big business, which sees the cost of financing the state as a threat to profitability. However, while the Tories reduced direct taxes on income and profits and cut the overall cost of welfare, they simultaneously increased indirect taxes on consumption, which tend to disfavour those from lower socioeconomic groups. Tory reforms also led to a reduction in spending on local services as borough councils were required to trim their budgets to meet new central government targets.

The strong state

These three examples demonstrate the importance the Conservatives attached to economic liberalism. The fact that such policies are now largely taken for granted by both the main parties suggests the extent to which New Right ideology represents a *hegemonic* strategy oriented towards a defence of the marketplace society. By themselves, however, these policies constitute only *one* aspect of New Right thinking, which would be incomplete without a neoconservative emphasis on self-reliance, authority and tradition. At the centre of modern conservatism is a preference for a strong state as a *framework within which a free economy can function.*

New Right conservatives view the state not as a guarantor of social welfare, but as a source of discipline and security in liberal–capitalist societies undergoing rapid social change. As we saw in Chapter 4, critics of the New Right use the term 'authoritarian populism' to suggest that the defence of individualism, economic liberalism and consumer choice is incompatible with a traditional conservative emphasis on authority, law and order, and discipline. Conservatives, however, deny this. They stress that the authoritarian emphasis of New Right ideology is designed to *contain* the contradictory forces unleashed by the free market.

Thatcherism and neoconservatism

This authoritarian tendency can be seen in the following examples of neoconservatism, which demonstrate the importance that neoconservatives attach to the preservation of social stability in a period of rapid social and economic change.

The dangers of excessive democracy

Socialist critics of representative democracy argue that, as the increasing obsolescence of existing political–economic institutions becomes apparent, the traditions of thought that have sustained democratic society will eventually lose their capacity to convey legitimacy. They insist that traditional forms of parliamentary democracy are in danger of being reduced to an 'empty shell of rhetoric' unless new democratic institutions are created.

Neoconservatives, on the contrary, stress that *too much* democracy is unhelpful because it encourages excessive demands on government (the issue of 'ungovernability' discussed above) and because it increases demands for *equal access to resources*. Like classical liberals, neoconservatives see democracy essentially as a device for choosing representatives and removing incompetent rulers. Democracy cannot be an open-ended mechanism for enforcing popular sovereignty, because such mechanisms risk undermining the fragile legitimacy of the existing (unequal) distribution of resources. For this reason, the Tories were keen to reduce the constraints that local and other forms of democracy exerted on the drive towards a market economy. This principally involved an attack on so-called 'Loony Left' councils that tried to use local government revenue to finance local services. In place of the old local rating system, the Conservatives introduced the community charge (poll tax), which was designed to break the link between wealth and local taxation by creating a flat-rate 'head tax' based on individuals rather than property.

For the Conservatives the main purpose of local government was not democracy but the efficient provision of services using cheaper private firms rather than more costly public sector workers. The main consequence of this was, however, to cut funding for local services and initiatives designed to help disadvantaged groups. Although there was intense opposition to these budget cuts from the left, the reforms restricted the extent to which socialist local authorities could frustrate the drive towards a deregulated market economy.

Law and order

A key area of concern for the Conservative Party was the preservation of law and order, particularly in relation to industrial disputes, property-related crime and political extremism/terrorism. The introduction of legislation regulating trade union activities in the early 1980s, the passage of the 1984/1988/1994 Criminal Justice Acts and the revision of the Official Secrets Act were the first of many pieces of legislation (all continued and updated under New Labour) designed to give the police and security forces more powers to deal with criminals and 'extremists'. Critics of the Conservatives argued that these new police powers constituted a threat to civil liberties. But Tory ministers insisted that they were necessary to clarify the precise powers of the police and to modernise the criminal justice system in the face of new and unprecedented pressures.

The importance of the Conservatives' law and order agenda as a constituent part of the new political consensus cannot be overestimated. In the 1980s and 1990s, the law and order agenda was politically popular and struck a chord with many voters tired of crime and social disorder. Like economic deregulation, the argument in favour of increased security gradually assumed a 'taken for granted' status: few within the political mainstream now question the idea of granting more powers to the state, even though such powers are difficult to monitor and control.

Family values

Another key policy initiative of the neoconservative right in the 1980s was the emphasis on family values, parental responsibility and personal morality. At the heart of neoconservative ideology is a belief that the traditional nuclear family should be defended as a bulwark against the corrosive effects of modernity. The family performs a distinct and vital function as the agency of primary sociali-sation, and neoconservatives argue that bad parenting is a source of major social problems, such as juvenile delinquency, disrespect for authority and criminality. They also argue that socialism and permissive liberalism are jointly responsible for undermining the integrity of the family. On the one hand, socialists are more willing to intervene in the private sphere of individuals: for example, by reducing parental choice over choice of schools. On the other hand, permissive liberals fail to appreciate the importance of authority and discipline as means of instilling respect and order in the younger generation.

Problems of modern conservatism

A central paradox of modern conservatism lies, therefore, in the dissonance between the neoliberal demand for risk acceptance and the traditional conser-vative demands for stability and continuity. Although, as argued in Chapter 4, modern conservatives have long since abandoned the corporatist vision of a cohesive organic society in which the freedom of the individual is balanced against duty and responsibility to the community, there is a discrepancy between the traditionalist defence of social stability and the modern conserva-tive defence of deregulated market capitalism.

A further problem for the New Right is that the attempt to *decrease* the coercive nature of the state tends to *increase* the coercive nature of the market. By requiring people to adapt to the changing needs of the marketplace society (and thus achieve independence from the state), economic coercion recreates incentives for social conformism and obedience to authority by linking prosperity and status to personal achievement within a competitive system of exchange. Individuals have little choice but to adapt to the impersonal authority of the market if they wish to progress in the new enterprise economy.

The contradictory legacy of the New Right

It is clear, therefore, that a potential source of tension in the New Right project lies in the conflict between support for economic freedom and a preference for social stability. It is also clear that the civil liberties of individuals may be jeopardised by the coercive power of the state in an attempt to secure the conditions necessary for economic liberty. The idea of using the state to 'roll back the frontiers of the state' not only is paradoxical, but also can lead to the possibility of governments *forcing* reluctant individuals to adapt to the impersonal authority of the market as a way of reducing the role of the public sector in the allocation of resources.

The question is, therefore, are the laissez-faire policies of the New Right compatible with a traditional conservative defence of the status quo? Or does the market unleash social forces that are hostile to, and ultimately destructive of, conservative values? To make sense of this question it is necessary to examine the contradictory impact of the New Right on society, before drawing some conclusions about the balance between neoliberalism and traditionalism in modern conservative ideology.

The impact of neoliberalism on the economy

The destabilising nature of market libertarianism can be seen in the impact of economic change on the structure of communities and traditional ways of life. An obvious example of this is the destruction of mining communities caused by the closure of the coal industry. The impact of the closure of the pits in the 1980s was catastrophic for communities that had no alternative source of employment, and the decline of the coal industry led to the decline of a whole way of life.

The decline of the traditional manufacturing sector, too, had a destabilising impact on society in general, increasing alienation and criminality among disadvantaged groups. The experience of mass unemployment increasingly polarised UK society into two nations, one more economically secure, the other more vulnerable and excluded. Despite the rhetoric of New Labour's 'stake-holder' ideology, this trend has continued since 1997.

A result of the conflict between economic freedom and social stability is the growing domination of the large supermarkets over the food industry. The large supermarket chains, which control most of the market, are placing increasing pressure on smaller retailers and independent farmers, who have no option but to adapt to prices and policies set by the main retailers. Although the growth of the major chains represents an economic success story (particularly for shareholders), the gradual disappearance of small-scale producers and local retailers tends to undermine the cohesiveness of local communities.

In a more general sense, however, the free market increases social mobility, which in turn uproots communities, reducing social cohesion and social stability. In the postwar era, workers might have expected to live a more stable existence, with a job for life and the certainty of a secure state pension. Yet, with the increasing rationalisation of working practices and less job security, it is harder for individuals and families to rely on comfortable certainties.

The impact of economic change on the family

Neoliberal economic policies have had a major impact on the family. Since the emergence of capitalism, the family has been required to adapt continually to economic development, which has resulted in the emergence of the small unit known as the nuclear family. Since the Second World War, the structure of the nuclear family has changed further, partly in response to feminist demands for women's emancipation, but also as a result of the changing structure of the labour market, which (except at the upper level) is no longer dominated by men. Increasingly, the economy requires efficient and compliant female workers to do jobs that may be less suitable for men, resulting in an increasing number of women choosing careers instead of marriage and motherhood. Although many working-class women have *always* been required to work, the changing structure of the labour market and the increasing cost of living mean that more middle-class and lower middle-class women, too, now have little choice but to work. In this sense, the old-fashioned conservative ideal of the 'stay-at-home' mother devoted to bringing up children is increasingly unrealistic.

The erosion of traditional authority

Economic liberalism has led to the erosion of traditional forms of authority by the impersonal nature of the market and the growth of materialism. Neoconservative New Right theorists advocate an authoritarian–populist agenda that highlights the cultural and spiritual decline of liberal–capitalist societies. From a neoconservative perspective, there is a contradiction between the economic rationality of Western society and the 'permissive social culture' which, it is argued, undermines the basis of rational organisation by fostering disrespect for authority, non-conformism and subversive attitudes. To deal with these problems, they advocate a return to faith, patriotism and 'family values', insisting that it is only through the 'normalising power' of tradition that liberal–capitalist societies can reclaim the moral foundations necessary to deal with the effects of rapid economic change.

There are clearly problems with this view, however, not least because the neoconservative call for a 'remoralisation' of society in accordance with a single core of ethical values is both arbitrary and implausible. Declining deference towards convention and tradition cannot simply be halted through legislation or a reassertion of social authority. The neoconservative assumption that the state can address social pathologies by requiring individuals to behave in specific ways is at odds with the traditional assumption that there must be limits to the use of state power to engineer social outcomes.

Although neoconservatives are quick to criticise decadence and permissiveness as the negative social consequences of modern individualism, one of the main sources of this trend is consumer capitalism itself, which fosters materialism and a belief in unrestricted freedom of choice.

Individualism

The New Right emphasis on the liberty of the individual appears to contradict the conservative defence of community and obligation. At the heart of traditional conservatism lies a belief in the importance of duty and responsibility in the conduct of human relations. Human beings are not simply atoms colliding in a morally neutral space; rather, they are all socialised into a network of concrete social and cultural relationships rooted in common historical experience. The bonds that constitute human relationships place obligations on the individual. Individuals cannot just be free to choose identities at will, for such arbitrary choice eventually undermines the moral fabric binding communities together.

As we have seen, conservatives are attached to customs and conventions as received ways of acting and being. Customs and conventions are seen as naturally evolving social phenomena that help to bind individuals to agreed ways of life.

One example of convention in everyday life is language, which is acquired by all individuals during their formative years and is regulated by rules of grammar, syntax and vocabulary. Conservatives see the tendency among young people to flout the received codes of language use as a threat to the established order. When people wantonly swear or adopt alien terms as substitutes for received forms of communication, they are seen to be rebelling against the authority of tradition, undermining the fragile consensus that binds society together.

Declining national sovereignty

The ideological shift of the Conservative Party from paternalistic Toryism to liberal Whiggism in recent decades has taken place against the backdrop of radical changes in the global market economy, which have forced governments around the world to relinquish old-fashioned ideas of political and economic sovereignty. With the exception of the most powerful states, governments can no longer 'act alone' in the world market, and economic decision making in the UK is closely determined by events in the USA and the European Union. This is a result of globalisation, which shifts and disperses authority away from central government to extraterritorial and subsidiary forms of governance, challenging the traditional political–territorial function of the state in the regulation of national economies. National governments can no longer claim full sovereignty over their territory, population and resources, for these are increasingly mobile and flexible in response to market forces. Hence, while conservatives seek to defend an indivisible concept of sovereignty, integration within the global economy has rendered the traditional concept of sovereignty redundant.

The paradoxical nature of the New Right

By ruthlessly liberalising and deregulating the UK economy, the Conservative Party temporarily succeeded in arresting the problem of the UK's 'managed decline' — although, as this short analysis demonstrates, this economic medicine was not without its side-effects. The ideological innovation of Thatcherism lay in its successful *populist* defence of middle-class values and interests in terms of a defence of 'middle England'. Thatcher instinctively believed in and projected the values of the 'honest, hard-working individual', self-reliant, dutiful and free from intellectual pretensions. This projection helped the Conservatives to broaden the class appeal of the party beyond its traditional constituency, and to capitalise on the weakness of the Labour Party, which was far too preoccupied by its own internal ideological divisions to challenge the hegemonic rise of the New Right.

Here we can see the paradoxical nature of the New Right as a populist alternative to egalitarian social engineering. This experiment was based on the view that the materialist ethos of self-enrichment, thrift and competitive individualism was sufficient to enable people from humble backgrounds to achieve social mobility: hard work and good character — rather than inherited social and economic capital — were what mattered.

The Thatcher experiment in social engineering in many ways ranks alongside Labour's experiment in social engineering in the 1960s, when the Wilson government tried to replace the tripartite education system with a new system of comprehensive schools. Just as Labour's education reforms in the 1960s failed to transform the class structure of UK society, however, so the Conservatives' market libertarianism ultimately failed to break down the division between middle-class and working-class culture. As George Schöpflin suggests (2000), in the 1960s Labour misunderstood that the origins of class lie not in education but in what Schöpflin terms a 'complex set of interrelated identities, which depend on one another for their reproduction. No direct assault will change this state of affairs'.

Thatcher set out to replace the complex determinants of class with a more straightforward *materialist* definition of status based on consumption and wealth: if one could contribute to wealth creation and prosperity, then one deserved a place in the 'favoured' nation of respectable citizens. The focus on material accumulation as the primary goal of independent individuals implied a tacit assault on the principle of inherited status and formal education as the main determinants of social class, which some observers saw as truly radical.

However, this quickly generated opposition among elites, who successfully deployed the centralised power of the state to resist any serious threat to the dominance of English class identity in the upper echelons of British society. These elites sought to portray aspirational lower-middle-class and working-class voters as unsophisticated *arrivistes* (or 'new rich'). As a result, the long-term impact of Thatcherism on the class structure of the UK was reduced.

It can be argued that class survives in the UK because the majority of people wish to perpetuate difference as a means of reinforcing identity and maintaining exclusion. Like the introduction of comprehensive education, the populist celebration of economic freedom at the heart of Thatcherism failed to reverse the deep-seated British attachment to class as a mechanism of differentiation and exclusion.

For Tory traditionalists, the New Right onslaught on the comfortable certainties of British life was unappealing. Many one-nation Tories supported Thatcher conditionally, believing that the market would, eventually, generate sufficient wealth to justify unfettered materialism. But many feared that the New Right assault on welfarism and community would backfire by creating expectations of social mobility that were unsustainable, and by increasing social polarisation.

In this they were proved partially correct: for many working-class and lower middle-class voters, the rhetoric of a 'property-owing democracy' turned out to be painfully hollow as mortgage rates increased in the early 1990s, forcing tens of thousands of new homeowners into a state of negative equity.

Furthermore, the New Right assumption that individuals should simply abandon their commitments to the community in favour of material gratification and self-interest was offensive to those traditionalists who preferred to see conservatism as a pragmatic worldview that draws its strength from an inclusive 'centrist' approach. Traditionalists were also troubled by the overtly ideological character of neoliberalism, which is dependent upon a set of questionable assumptions about human behaviour that are largely (but by no means completely) absent from one-nation ideology.

Debate on the impact of Thatcherism on UK politics and society remains a subject of great controversy:

- Some observers argue that its impact has been limited. They point to the fact that the UK is still a welfare state, that British people still place enormous value on public institutions such as the BBC and the National Health Service, and that — despite budget cuts — the 'overall level of taxation and public expenditure relative to the size of the economy was not very different when Thatcher left office than when she became prime minister' (Grant, 2003).

- Others, however, argue that while British voters still value public institutions, they are increasingly unwilling to pay for them through taxation. This reflects the influence of neoliberal ideology, which has become more widely accepted since the 1980s, not just among Conservative voters, but among supporters of New Labour, which has preserved and extended Conservative policies on income tax and inflation.

Assessing the balance between liberal and traditional aspects of UK conservatism

The real legacy of Thatcherism lies in the fact that Thatcher initiated a long-term process of structural adjustment designed to address the legitimacy crisis of the Keynesian welfare state. Neoliberalism is now a central aspect of the post-socialist consensus, and both main parties accept the superiority of market-based solutions over state ownership and regulation. Thatcher's detractors argue that she undermined the very basis of UK conservatism; but to her defenders, she was

an indefatigable campaigner against statist socialism, which is now a discredited model of economic organisation. Loyalists emphasise her charismatic appeal as a no-nonsense leader who preferred to confront problems head on rather than indulge in traditional 'fudge' measures.

Thatcher's long-term impact on the development of UK conservatism has, however, been much more complex and further complicated by subsequent leaders such as John Major and William Hague, who tried to modify Thatcherism to suit a changing political environment. John Major tried — and failed — to stamp his authority on the party by promoting pro-Europeans such as Ken Clarke and Michael Heseltine, while simultaneously trying to restrain the activities of die-hard Thatcher loyalists in the No Turning Back Group. This group wanted to preserve and extend Thatcher's negative approach to the EU integration, particularly her hostility towards the Franco-German axis and the Maastricht Treaty.

John Major was personally undermined by behind-the-scenes interference from Margaret Thatcher, who contemptuously dismissed the idea of 'Majorism' as an alternative form of conservative ideology. Yet the political and economic problems that blighted his premiership should not blind us to the *underlying* ideological tension within Tory ideology that persists to the present day. This tension stems from a deep-rooted conflict between the party's liberal/ modernising tendency, which advocates individualism and social progressivism, and its authoritarian/traditionalist tendency, which is concerned with fiscal prudence, social discipline and national sovereignty.

The Major years

After the fall of Margaret Thatcher in 1990, the Conservative Party entered a new era of conflict between those who wanted to moderate the New Right agenda pursued in the 1980s and those Thatcher loyalists who wanted to consolidate her achievements. Critics of John Major argue that he failed to develop an independent agenda of his own, and that ideologically the Tories continued during the 1990s with a kind of 'Thatcherism Mark II'. There is some truth to this accusation, although John Major did manage to defy his Thatcherite critics within the party over Europe. Three issues dominated politics during the Major years: economic recession, Europe and government sleaze.

Economic recession

Although like Margaret Thatcher a fiscal conservative from a modest social background, Major was uncomfortable with the radical market libertarianism of figures such as John Redwood, Norman Lamont and Peter Lilley. Major preserved the policy of reduced income tax and fiscal prudence, but was faced with rising inflation and a balance of payments deficit at precisely the moment when the Treasury and the Bank of England were trying to stabilise the pound in the exchange rate mechanism. The collapse of the pound on 'Black Wednesday' in September 1992 triggered an economic recession and a collapse in the housing market, which undermined the Conservatives' reputation as the party of economic competence. Even though the economy recovered during the mid-1990s under the Conservatives, the voters punished the party in the 1997 elections, ending 18 years of unbroken Tory rule.

Europe

John Major became prime minister at a point when the UK government was uncertain about how to deal with EU integration and the consequences of German reunification. Major signed the Maastricht Treaty, but failed to convince the Eurosceptics in his party of the value of further EU integration. After the experience of Black Wednesday, a hard-core of right-wing MPs opposed any further compromise on the single currency, demanding an immediate referendum on entry as a means of forcing Major's hand. Instead, this forced the prime minister to confront his critics in the cabinet, whom he accused of treachery. This was followed by several high-profile departures from the cabinet and a leadership contest that only partially reinstated Major's battered authority. The withdrawal of the party whip from the Maastricht rebels (who voted against the treaty in 1993) meant that Major gradually lost his majority in parliament, which forced him to rely on the support of the Ulster Unionists in order to pass legislation.

Government sleaze

Amid the storm of controversy over recession and EU integration, the Conservatives also suffered a humiliating series of public relations disasters caused by revelations of sex scandals and financial impropriety among Tory MPs and abuses of power by ministers. The most famous example of this was the 'Cash for Questions' saga involving Neil Hamilton and Mohammad al-Fayed, although this was somewhat overshadowed by the more salacious stories in the media concerning the private lives of ministers — just as the government was trying to put into effect a 'Back to Basics' campaign designed to reassert traditional social and moral values. This undermined John Major's credibility and increased popular disillusion at the apparent hypocrisy of the Conservatives.

The 1997 election and after

After 1997 the Conservative Party found itself in the political wilderness, reduced to a rump of 165 MPs without a single MP outside England. The crushing nature of the defeat (see Table 5.1) forced the party into a period of soul-searching in order to navigate a route back to the political mainstream.

Table 5.1 **UK general election, 1997**

Party	Seats	Gains	Losses	Net gain/ loss	Seats (%)	Votes (%)	Votes	+/–
New Labour	418	145	–	+145	63	43.2	13,518,167	+8.8
Conservative	165	–	178	–178	25	30.7	9,600,943	–10.2
Liberal Democrat	46	30	2	+28	7	16.8	5,242,947	–1.0
Referendum Party	–	–	–	–	0	2.6	811,849	n/a
SNP	6	3	–	+3	1	2.0	621,550	+0.1

Yet the loss of so many senior Tory MPs provided an opportunity for the youthful William Hague to enter the race for the leadership. He represented the modernising tendency within the Conservative Party, which wanted to draw a line under the recent past and develop a new programme of progressive conservative policies in tune with the views of mainstream voters. With support among different sections of the parliamentary party, Hague was selected in preference to heavyweight rivals such as Ken Clarke.

As a moderniser, William Hague represented a new broom, introducing changes to the organisation of the party and the process of leadership selection. Ideologically, he portrayed himself as a libertarian conservative opposed to what many saw as the overweening political correctness and 'nanny-state' policies of New Labour. Hague's strategy was to try to win back sceptical voters by extending the Conservatives' libertarian agenda to the sphere of social policy, emphasising both economic freedom *and* personal freedom. This was designed to counter the stuffy, moralising image of the Tories in the 1980s and 1990s. However, there was an inherent contradiction in Hague's strategy: by relinquishing their image as the party of authority and tradition, the Tories risked alienating core supporters in a desperate effort to win back swing voters who had abandoned the party for New Labour in 1997.

Hague acknowledged this contradiction and rapidly changed his tone. In place of libertarianism, he began to propose a new form of 'common-sense conservatism', emphasising the importance of duty to the community, law and order, marriage and self-reliance. Hague therefore tried to resolve the contradiction at the heart of conservative ideology between bourgeois individualism and traditionalism. However, this agenda had only limited appeal among the electorate and did little to boost the party's support in the 2001 general election. Resolution of this contradiction eluded his successor, Iain Duncan Smith, who also suffered from a stuffy, old-fashioned image in the media. Duncan Smith accepted that the Tories were seen by many as the 'nasty party', but his lack of popular appeal and failure to provide an alternative to New Labour led to his own replacement by Michael Howard in 2003.

Michael Howard's leadership of the party was similarly characterised by ideological uncertainty and weak political strategy. In many respects, Howard represented a return to the statesmanlike preference for pragmatic 'high politics', but the effect of this was to leave voters uncertain about what he represented. He began his leadership with a inclusive commitment to govern in the name of 'all Britain and all Britons', although this idea did not last long. Howard also campaigned for a short time with a call for social justice, but this commitment was equally short-lived.

The only aspect of Tory policy that caught the popular imagination in the 2005 election was the party's proposal to impose tight controls on immigration. This appealed to core voters, and possibly prevented a further loss of votes to the UK Independence Party. But mainstream voters were put off by the authoritarian–populist tone and opportunist nature of Conservative strategy (which was inspired by an Australian campaign adviser), and Michael Howard failed to win back sufficient seats in May 2005 to justify his continued leadership of the party. The Tories were adversely affected by boundary changes and shifts in electoral participation and demographic voting patterns, and, consequently, the 2005 election was a much greater success for the Liberal Democrats, who received almost 75% of the total number of votes for the Conservative Party. This led some observers to conclude that the Conservatives would also benefit from a more proportional voting system.

Like William Hague, Howard tended to zigzag between libertarianism (focusing on individual choice and economic freedom), and authoritarianism (focusing on law and order, immigration and national sovereignty). Despite the increasing unpopularity of Tony Blair over the Iraq War, Howard failed to inspire the Conservative Party to transform itself into a new broad-based coalition of the centre-right.

The 2005 leadership election

The ideological division within modern conservative ideology was visible in the 2005 Tory leadership contest between David Davis and David Cameron. As

candidate of the right, Davis represented the tax-cutting, authoritarian–populist, anti-European trend within conservatism. Like Thatcher, he is the product of a grammar school education, a man who worked hard to overcome adversity and rise to the top. For this reason, he appealed to party members inclined towards a philosophy of self-reliance, hard work and personal discipline, though his appeal did not go far enough. He tried to rehabilitate the idea of the successful man from humble origins who had risen above class and inherited inequality to become leader of the Tory Party. But in an age of personality politics, his lack of charisma undermined his candidacy, as party members opted for a younger man with broader appeal.

By contrast, David Cameron hails from a privileged social background, having been educated at Eton and Oxford, and has struggled to shake off a slightly 'patrician' image which reflects this background. As the candidate of the modernising wing of the party, however, he represents a more liberal social agenda, and has moved to take advantage of New Labour's weak record on environmental issues. Although he made few explicit policy commitments during the campaign (which some commentators saw as a rational move), he won because he appealed to voters put off by Davis's absence of personality. He was seen as the candidate most likely to win back wavering swing voters disillusioned with New Labour and anxious about the possible consequences of a government led by Gordon Brown.

It is clear, however, that — like Tony Blair — Cameron may be something of a political 'chameleon' without concrete political or ideological views. In this respect, he inherits the mantle of the pragmatic conservative, for whom ideology

David Davis and David Cameron campaigning for the Tory leadership

and policy are less important than 'vision', presentation and leadership style. Combined with a flamboyant social profile and a youthful appearance, Cameron's campaign was in some respects a triumph of style over substance, as he offered the Conservative Party faithful a sense of hope and purpose in the dying days of the Blair era.

Conclusion

The purpose of this chapter has been to assess whether the UK Conservatives still constitute an authentic conservative party. It has been shown that the adoption of a two-nation strategy under Margaret Thatcher represented a radical departure from old-style Tory paternalism, although Thatcher's predecessor, Edward Heath, had also tried (and failed) to develop a market libertarian agenda in the early 1970s.

In many respects, the absorption of New Right ideology undermined the traditional character of the Conservatives as an inclusive centre-right coalition. However, it is clear that the Tories had long since abandoned the 'organic' theory of society popular among nineteenth-century conservatives, in favour of a more pragmatic defence of economic prosperity and national sovereignty.

By adopting a radical free-market stance, the Tories have not abandoned their claim to be the traditional defenders of faith, family and nation; however, they have relinquished the inclusive centrist values associated with one-nation conservative ideology. This reflects a shift away from 'benevolent elitism' towards 'authoritarian populism', as a result of which it is the market rather than the state which determines economic outcomes.

In attempting to define a new route for the Conservative Party, David Cameron has been careful to avoid making explicit or radical statements on economic policy. However, he has suggested that the Tories should try to depict themselves as defenders of liberal values, rather than position the party too far to the right. Although the two main parties agree broadly on a neoliberal *economic* agenda and an authoritarian *social* agenda, the Conservatives clearly wish to present themselves as defenders of liberty and choice, opposing the 'tax-and-spend', 'nanny-state' policies of New Labour.

On balance, it is clear that the Tories are still a conservative political party, albeit one that has changed radically since the 1970s. The party has attempted to modernise its image by adopting a more socially liberal agenda to match its neoliberal economic policies, but there is no indication yet that the Tories are prepared to relinquish their claim to represent the discontented voters of middle England.

Chapter 5

Task 5.1

Read Source A and complete the questions that follow.

Source A

The allure of individual freedom as the icing on the Thatcherite cake is firmly anchored in its ideological structure. ...This decontestation of freedom is cemented to prosperity and to personal responsibility, thus offering the financial inducements of the market while absolving the public domain
5   from the onus of guaranteeing those fruits of free choice. Choice and independence are decontested in close proximity to the values of economic independence and economic participation, through the use of perimeter practices involving privatisation, the sale of council houses, and the proliferation of share ownership. The reduction of choice to the economic sphere is
10 presented as strengthening the family and as checking state power. It also entails exposure of newly privatised companies 'to the full commercial disciplines of the customer'. The elevation of the individual as customer or client assists in realigning the relationship between the economic and the political spheres.

Michael Freeden, *Ideologies and Political Theory*, OUP (1998)

(a) What is meant by 'freedom is cemented to prosperity' in Thatcherite ideology (lines 2–3)? Why should freedom be dependent on economic success?

(b) In what ways are privatisation, share ownership, and the sale of council houses inducements to individuals to achieve economic independence (lines 8–9)?

(c) Why are New Right conservatives anxious to limit choice and freedom to the economic sphere? (line 9)

(d) In what sense does Thatcherism alter the 'relationship between the economic and the political spheres' (lines 13–14)?

Guidance

As we have seen, there is a link between the Conservatives' neoliberal agenda (economic laissez faire, deregulation, privatisation etc.) and the party's neoconservative agenda (law and order, family values, anti-radicalism etc.).

At the centre of New Right ideology is a belief that free-market capitalism promotes prosperity and self-reliance — that individuals who strive for economic independence will stand on their own two feet rather than become a burden on the state.

Although the laissez-faire philosophy of neoliberalism appears to contradict the conservative preference for a strong state, Thatcher and her supporters were keen to reassert economic freedom within the framework of a cohesive, ordered society. Choice and freedom are to be realised primarily through consumerism rather than through an abstract conception of rights.

Task 5.2

Copy and complete the following table to explain the importance of the concepts listed in modern conservatism.

Authority	
Social cohesion	
Tradition	
Self-reliance	
Personal responsibility	
Economic freedom	
Individualism	
Patriotism	

Guidance

Think about the distinction between traditional and modern conservatism outlined in preceding chapters. How far have the Conservatives shifted away from their former emphasis on social cohesion and social stability? Is the party still ostensibly a *conservative* party — that is, one committed to the pragmatic defence and gradual evolution of established institutions and ways of life? Or does pragmatism for modern conservatives simply imply adaptation to the changing needs of the market?

Chapter 5

Useful websites

- On the development of Thatcherism, see:
  http://en.wikipedia.org/wiki/Thatcherism
  www.bbc.co.uk/history/timelines/england/pwar_thatcherism.shtml
  www.lrb.co.uk/v20/n24/clar03_.html
- On Conservative politics in the UK, see:
  www.conservatives.com/

Further reading

- Grant, W. (2003) 'Economic policy', *Developments in British Politics*, no.7.
- Green, E. H. H. (2002) *Ideologies of Conservatism: Conservative Political Ideas in the Twentieth Century*, Oxford University Press.
- Jessop, B. et al. (1988) *Thatcherism: A Tale of Two Nations*, Polity Press.
- Levitas, R. (2005) *The Inclusive Society?: Social Exclusion and New Labour*, Palgrave Macmillan.
- Rancière, J. (1999) *Disagreement: Politics and Philosophy*, University of Minnesota Press.
- Schöpflin, G. (2000) 'Englishness: citizenship, ethnicity and class, in G. Schöpflin, *Nations, Identity, Power: The New Politics of Europe*, C. Hurst & Co. Ltd.